TAI CHI & QIGONG

ENERGY HEALING FOR ADULTS AND SENIORS

太极

太極

POWERFUL EXERCISES, LESSONS AND TRAININGS, CULTIVATE YOUR INNER QI FLOW, IMPROVE CONCENTRATION, SLEEP & MOOD AND DEEPEN YOUR MEDITATION

CHEN SONG

Tai Chi & Qigong Energy Healing For Adults And Seniors

Powerful Exercises, Lessons And Trainings, Cultivate Your Inner Qi Flow, Improve Concentration, Sleep & Mood And Deepen Your Meditation

Chen Song

QIGONG
For Beginners

CHINESE HEALING ENERGY FROM WITHIN

PROVEN PRACTICES & EXERCISES TO CULTIVATE YOUR CHI FLOW, REDUCE STRESS & IMPROVE YOUR SLEEP THROUGH TRAINING & MEDITATION (FOR ADULTS & SENIORS)

CHEN SONG

Table of Contents

Introduction

We live in a world that is constantly stressful, always changing, and usually throwing challenges and problems our way. Not a day goes by without some kind of issue to handle for many people. Put simply, the entire process can become exhausting.

Yet, we're missing out on the good stuff by constantly battling problems, tiredness, and stress, right?

Life is for living. There are so many amazing experiences to be had, and we're missing them because we're too focused on life's negative aspects.

Does this sound like a similar story?

If you're nodding along, then you're not alone. There are so many people out there who are going through the same thing as you right now. You're tired, stressed, fed up with feeling challenged. You want to take control of your health, but you're not sure how. You have so much information flying at you from all directions that you just can't concentrate and focus on the things you want to spend time focusing on.

Of course, there are many different avenues you can go down to try and take back control of your life, but sometimes the natural elements are much more effective. They're also far easier to master, and you can start right away.

With that in mind, have you heard of QiGong?

Pronounced' chee-gong', this ancient Chinese healing method has been used for centuries to manage the problem we've just talked about. The issue? People assume that you need to go down the route of medical intervention to solve problems.

Now, in some cases, that's certainly to be recommended. You should always listen to the advice of your doctor, for sure. But in some cases, it's not medicine you need but the ability to harness the power all around you. That's precisely what qi-gong does.

Forget Your Preconceptions

The biggest issue with any holistic treatment method is often a lack of trust. But, let's be truthful here. Traditional Chinese medicine has been around longer than any of us. We're talking hundreds of years here. It's been used by countless people for many different problems and has yielded a lot of success.

If you want QiGong to work for you, you need to believe in it. You need to have faith that it will work for you, and you need to put your all into making it a success. If you can do that, you're already halfway there. Negative thinking will drastically affect your success, so by ensuring that you're not already damaging your efforts, you're protecting what you're about to achieve.

Of course, at this point, you might not have the first idea of what QiGong is. You just know that it's something that can help you with your problems. That's fine at this stage. This book is going to give you all the information you need to learn about QiGong and understand what you need to do to harness its power.

But first, any stereotypical thought or far-fetched idea needs to be pushed firmly out of your mind. From this point on, it's positive thinking all the way.

First Thing First, What Exactly is QiGong?

Ah, the million-dollar question.

In the coming chapters, we will outline everything you need to know about QiGong, but first, you need to know what you're getting yourself into.

QiGong is an ancient Chinese medicine method for healing. It uses breathing, movements, and meditation to help calm the mind, soothe the body, improve flexibility and coordination, boost focus, and give you a better picture of health. QiGong covers not only your physical health, but your mental, emotional, and spiritual health too.

Those busy lives we all lead have a nasty habit of causing us to rush from one thing to another, never allowing ourselves the time we need to just 'be.' As a result, your chakras or meridians can become blocked or unaligned. When that happens, chi, or energy, is unable to flow freely throughout the body. This can lead to health problems and a generally 'blocked' feeling.

QiGong helps to move that energy again while giving you the confidence and serenity to know you can handle any problem that life throws at you.

Of course, QiGong isn't something you're going to master overnight. If you're keen to go on this journey, you need to put forth the time and effort. You need to start from scratch and be willing to open your mind to the possibilities before you. Those negative thoughts need to be pushed aside, and you need to dedicate yourself to self-care.

If you can do that, you'll soon be able to grab the benefits that QiGong offers.

Wait, Isn't QiGong the Same as Tai Chi?

That's a common misconception, but no, they're not the same.

You've undoubtedly seen Tai Chi in action before, probably in a Hollywood movie or drama series. It's a very popular deal and something that can bring you many benefits. Many of the benefits Tai Chi offers mirror those given by QiGong, but the actual process isn't the same. The differences are subtle, but they're still there.

Tai chi is about holding postures, but QiGong is about a flow of movements that automatically happen.

It doesn't sound very clear, for sure, but everything is going to become crystal clear in the coming chapters.

You're going to learn the ins and outs of QiGong and all about yin and yang. Then, we will give you more information on the benefits and how you can use QiGong to boost your health. From there, we're going to delve deeply into how to practice QiGong itself. You'll learn about the body areas that need to be corrected before it's time to get practical. From meditation to diet, visualization exercises to breathing, you'll find step-by-step guides to help you to build your confidence in a strong and steady manner.

It's true that QiGong isn't going to slam into your life like a hurricane. It's not going to make a significant difference tomorrow just because you've started to read about it today, but over a short amount of time, you'll see differences that start to pick up the pace.

Right now, you need to give yourself a pat on the back. You're about to embark upon a journey of discovery and self-improvement. Many people don't even bother to learn something new, let alone do something that will improve their lives. You're doing more than that; you're keen to go further and live a life free of stress. QiGong will give you a coping mechanism to lean on when life gets tough, while also allowing you to reap health benefits beyond your imagination right now.

So, after that pat on the back, you simply need to turn the page and start your exhilarating journey into the wonderful world of QiGong.

Chapter 1:
The History Of QiGong And The Purpose Behind It

Welcome to the first chapter. By reading this far, you've shown a desire to not only want to learn about QiGong but a desire to implement it into your own life. That's a great start!

In this chapter, we're going to give you a complete overview of what QiGong is, where it came from, what it is used for, and we're also going to talk about yin, yang, and the elements. By the end of this chapter, you'll have a much clearer view of what you can expect from your journey.

What QiGong Really Is

Before you can begin using QiGong yourself, you need a clear view of what it is and how it's going to work out for you. Nothing is ideal for every single person on the planet, but the great thing about QiGong is that you can adapt it to your needs and requirements.

So, first, let's explore QiGong in a bit more detail.

QiGong is pronounced "chee gong." Qi means 'energy,' and the gong part is about creating it or cultivation. So, in essence, QiGong is the cultivation of vital energy.

This ancient healing method was developed thousands of years ago in Ancient China, and it forms an integral part of traditional Chinese medicine. Of course, it does look a little like Tai Chi on the outside, and although we've touched upon that briefly already, we will delve deeper into it later on so you can understand the critical differences in a bit more detail. That's another vital part of the story - you don't need to be confused with another particular type of healing; you need to choose the one that suits you and then focus on it entirely.

QiGong uses exercises to cultivate and optimize the flow of energy through the mind and body, and the spirit. As a result, your health and wellbeing are improved and maintained over the long-term. QiGong also uses meditation, visualization, and breathing exercises to cultivate that all-important energy. It's a natural method that doesn't involve anything other than what your body can do on its own - the power of mind over matter, nourishing your body with the right foods, and using your breath and posture.

There are different types of QiGong, which we'll cover shortly, but in the majority of them, you will use:

- Slow and deep breathing, involving targeted breathing from the abdomen and using specific sounds at the same time
- Gentle movements that smoothly move from one to the next, helping to relax the mind and body
- Visualization to focus the mind and attention

Within this, there are two primary forms of QiGong - active and passive.

Active QiGong is also known as dynamic, and this is the part that involves movement of the body. Passive QiGong is also known as meditative, and that is the part that uses your breath, visualization, and meditation exercises. You will combine both forms when following your personal QiGong journey.

The idea is that both the active and passive methods will help you to ensure the free flow of energy and its relationship with the elements around you. In that case, spirit, matter, and energy are aligned, and balance is achieved.

A Brief History of QiGong

It is thought that QiGong was created around 2500 years ago; however, it was documented in Taoist scripture in 600AD. Even before that time, there was evidence of practices that looked a lot like QiGong.

It wasn't until around the 1940s that QiGong started to go mainstream and was used away from the traditional villages in rural China. At this time, traditional Chinese medicine was becoming more focused, and people were starting to recognize the benefits it could bring. This was further pushed to the fore as tourism within China began to boom, therefore allowing more people to become exposed to different medicinal methods. As Chinese people moved around the world, they also educated people from other walks of life about their ancient practices.

Of course, over time, QiGong has changed and evolved. There are several different types of QiGong nowadays, which we'll cover in more detail shortly. However, QiGong is also part of Chinese martial arts, using the cultivation of energy in that regard too.

These days, QiGong is practiced globally, by people from all different walks of life. Each person who chooses to practice QiGong does so for their own specific reasons. It may be because they want to use it for exercise or to increase flexibility. Perhaps they want to use it as a de-stressing tool, to reduce anxiety and depression, or for general self-healing. Of course, some people use it for training in martial arts too.

As we move through the first few chapters of this book, you'll start to identify your own reasons for wanting to use QiGong, and by harnessing your 'why,' you'll find the motivation to keep moving toward and learning more.

Exploring The Branches And Structure of QiGong

We know that QiGong uses many different parts to create the whole, but before you move into your first steps into the healing method, you need to understand the structure and the branches involved. That's what we're going to cover here.

The main structure of QiGong involves, as we've mentioned, breathing, mental training, and physical movement. All of this is based upon the Chinese healing philosophy and includes dynamic, meditative, and static activities.

Let's delve further into these three pillars of QiGong.

Static Training

The static part of QiGong is about holding the poses. Again, this is a little like yoga, so if you've ever used yoga before or you're a regular yoga enthusiast, you already have a head start to some degree. As with yoga, you will be highly aware of your breath during the poses, so you're able to move a little deeper and cultivate energy.

Dynamic Training

The dynamic elements of QiGong include movement that flows from one to the other in a fluid manner. These movements are choreographed carefully, and you use them in alignment with your breath, a little like you would in yoga. You're also carefully aware of individual movements, so they flow carefully from one to the next, without any interruption in the cultivation and flow of energy.

Meditation

This is the hardest part for many people, but meditation is actually far more straightforward than you might think. It simply requires practice. Focusing on your breath is a form of meditation in some way, as is visualization, another critical element, and pillar of

QiGong. You will also use mantras and focus on ensuring stillness of mind.

Alongside the above elements, you may also choose to use other aids, such as changing your diet, using herbs, or even massage. In regular QiGong, diet and herbs are pretty standard, whereas massage tends to be more common in QiGong used for martial arts purposes.

Of course, we have mentioned there are different types of QiGong, and you need to be aware of those too, as they differ slightly from one another. In this book, we will focus on the basics of getting started in QiGong, but as you become more au fait with it, you'll be able to specialize at some point in the future.

The main types of QiGong include:

- Medical or health QiGong
- Intellectual or scholarly QiGong
- Longevity or vitality QiGong
- Spiritual QiGong
- Martial or warrior QiGong

Understanding your reason for doing QiGong will help you to move into the best type for you.

Medical or health QiGong is probably the most common. This is used to help alleviate pain and chronic health conditions. This type of QiGong works hand in hand with other Chinese medicine methods, such as acupuncture. This type of QiGong is preferable for people who want to help alleviate such problems, including anxiety and depression.

Longevity or vitality is used for improving flexibility and bodily strength. It can also be used in fitness, so if you're training for an event, this type of QiGong may help you. Of course, the name also implies that you may be able to live longer by using this type of QiGong, and by building body strength that's thought to be a possibility!

Intellectual or scholarly QiGong is about boosting focus and memory. It can also help you to be less indecisive and more confident in your choices. Some people also believe that it can improve your luck, but of course, nothing has been proven.

Martial or warrior QiGong is a type of QiGong that focuses on speed, motivation, agility, and stamina. It's an excellent option for people who want to boost their clarity of mind, courage, and the ability to thrive in pressurized situations. The name denotes martial arts, and these are all elements that an athlete in these arts would need.

The last type is spiritual QiGong, which brings together mind, body, and spirit. It is about awareness and clarity of mind and for those who want to open their minds to spiritual awakening.

As you can see, a couple of the different types of QiGong overlap; you may want to improve your health and focus. That's fine; you can easily combine the two as it simply comes down to using different poses and visualization exercises. We will learn far more about that as we move through the book and arrive at the practical sections.

For now, you need this thorough overview so you know exactly what you're getting into, what you can get out of it, and how it can work for you in your daily life.

The Elements, The Yin And The Yang

Another fundamental principle in QiGong is yin and yang. We also need to talk about the elements and how they work hand in hand with the yin and yang principles.

Everyone has seen the yin and yang symbol; this is the black and white circle with one curved section in black, the other side in white, and an alternative color dot in the center of each side. It has long been a fashion symbol used in modern society, but it's about far more than that. Yin and yang is an essential principle in ancient Chinese philosophy and forms the basis of all traditional Chinese medicine methods.

The idea is that all things exist separately, but they're also connected despite being opposite. For instance, men and women are yin and yang. They're separate, but they're connected. Older adults and young people are separate, but they're connected through family ties. It's the idea that opposites attract because those differences work hand in hand and actually work to complement one another.

This principle is nothing new; it's been around since around the 3rd century BC, possibly even earlier than that. The yin and yang image shows you that the core color, e.g., white on the right hand side, still requires a dot of black in the middle because they complement one another. Neither yin nor yang is better than the other; they're equal in importance and status. If yin increases, so does yang, and vice versa. They can't exist without one another, and the balance must be equal in order for balance to be achieved.

In QiGong, an equal balance between the yin and yang elements ensures balance and therefore means that you're getting the benefits of the practice overall.

Let's take a look at the characteristics of both yin and yang.

Yin

The characteristics of yin are:

- Feminine energy

- The color black and generally dark
- Passive
- Associated with the moon and earth
- Cold temperatures
- The element of water
- The direction north
- Old age
- Even numbers
- Yin energy peaks during the winter
- Provides energy to everything
- Tiger
- Associated with the liver, heart, spleen, lungs, and kidneys

Yang

The characteristics of yang are:

- Masculine energy
- The element of fire
- Creativity
- Associated with the sun and heaven
- The color white and light
- The direction south
- Warm temperatures
- Youth
- Odd numbers
- Dragon
- Yang energy peaks during the summer
- Associated with the gallbladder, stomach, small and large intestines, and the bladder
- Provides form to everything

If we look at the human body regarding yin and yang energy, yang encompasses bodily functions, whereas the things required for functions to work, e.g., blood, fluids, etc., are yin. When the body functions correctly, i.e., both the yin and yang elements are working together to ensure smooth running, energy is created (qi).

In terms of QiGong, the movements, meditations, breathing, and visualization exercises work hand in hand to help align yin and yang and create qi.

We now need to use the yin and yang principle and bring elements into the mix.

The natural world is vital in any form of traditional Chinese medicine. Nature brings tranquility and calms, while an equal balance between the elements helps to boost the movement of energy. In this regard, we need to think about wood, earth, fire, metal, and water, which are paired with yin and yang organs.

- Wood is associated with the liver and gallbladder
- Earth is associated with the spleen and stomach
- Fire is associated with the heart and small intestine
- Metal is associated with the lungs and large intestine
- Water is associated with the kidney and bladder

Yin and yang come into this because all of these organs function on their own, yet they're working together to ensure healthy balance within the body. When these five phases and elements are in alignment, qi is generated and flows freely throughout the body.

How is all of this created? By using the dynamic, static, and meditative pillars of QiGong. By dedicating yourself to these practices, both yin and yang will be equal, and the elements will align to bring harmony and balance.

Points to Remember

Now, we can appreciate that at this point, you're probably wondering how all of this is going to work for you. It's a lot to take in. Don't worry if, at this stage, you're feeling a little overwhelmed. It's very normal. You're learning something new and probably something that, up until now, has been very alien to you. As you learn more, it will click into place. But, you must take your time and understand that you need to place dedication and time toward it to bring QiGong into your life. If you can do that, it will bring you many benefits.

The main points to remember from this chapter are:

- QiGong is an ancient Chinese medicine practice
- It has been around for at least 2500 years and possibly even before that
- QiGong is pronounced 'chee gong,' and it is about cultivating energy that flows freely throughout the body for optimum health and wellbeing
- There are different types of QiGong, including medical (health), longevity, intellectual, martial, and spiritual QiGong
- QiGong uses movement, posture, breath, meditation, and visualization in dynamic, static, and meditative phases
- Exploring your reason for embarking upon QiGong will help you to stay motivated and focus your attention on the poses that will give you the desired outcome
- Yin and yang are about opposites that work together to bring harmony
- Yin and yang form part of QiGong
- Yin is about energy, yang is about form, but they're both required to create qi (energy)
- The elements are connected to both yin and yang and help to boost your efforts
- Following the dynamic, static, and meditative practices of QiGong will help you to balance both yin and yang and find balance.

Chapter 2:
How QiGong Will Help You Live a Life of Happiness And Wellbeing

You know what QiGong is, where it came from, and the basics of yin and yang. You've already taken a giant leap toward incorporating QiGong into your life. But, you're probably wondering what exactly is in it for you. You know it has benefits, and you know that it can improve your health and wellbeing, but how exactly? What is it about QiGong that actually helps you to be healthier, and what does it target?

In this chapter, we're going to give you a push in the right direction. We're going to outline the main benefits of QiGong and give you a brief understanding of why it works for each particular benefit. Remember, QiGong has its doubters, and you don't need to be one of them if you want it to help you; that means debunking any doubts and keeping everything clear in your mind.

The Many Benefits of QiGong

Nobody would practice QiGong if it didn't bring major benefits, right? The same goes for other similar practices, such as Tai Chi, acupuncture, and even yoga. It has to bring you something that makes it worthwhile. Otherwise, surely you're just wasting your time. But, QiGong isn't a waste of time. It has countless benefits to your health and wellbeing.

Let's take a look at the main ones.

Loosens The Muscles

QiGong helps to promote relaxation, but that doesn't just mean relaxation of the mind, but the body too. We tend to hold a lot of tension in our muscles without realizing it, resulting in aches and pains. When you use QiGong on a regular basis, you're relaxed and tense muscles will be loosened.

Strengthens Bodily Organs

You'll remember in our last chapter, we talked about yin and yang and that each has specific organs it is responsible for. QiGong helps to realign and unblock energy problems, which allows yin and yang to be in balance. When this happens, your organs work as they're supposed to. It's also down to the exercise you're getting as you move through the poses and the lower stress levels the practice creates.

Helps to Build Muscle Power

You might wonder how QiGong helps to build muscle power if it's such a gentle endeavor. Anyone can do QiGong; you don't have to be particularly fit to start. But, as you move through the poses and keep learning more, you'll notice that your muscles become stronger and supple, and you're able to keep going for longer. The same goes for any type of exercise, which QiGong still is.

Stronger Nerves

Chronic pain is sometimes down to nerve pain more than anything else. QiGong helps to boost bodily strength and can help to reduce chronic pain, but it can also boost nerve strength which contributes toward optimum health and wellbeing throughout the whole body.

Slows Down Your Breathing Rate

Again, this is down to relaxation and less stress. When you breathe too fast, you're breathing in a shallow manner. This doesn't allow vital oxygen to get around the body as it should. By relaxing, learning how to control your breath, and breathing from the right place, you're able to ensure oxygen and nutrients make it to where they need to go. This can also help with respiratory problems such as asthma and bronchitis.

Increases Bone Density

Strong bones are very important for health, but as we age, our bones tend to weaken. This is particularly a problem for women as the amount of estrogen in the body starts to reduce in older age. This can cause conditions such as osteoporosis, or brittle bones. QiGong can help to increase bone density and strength, therefore reducing the chances of this problem occurring.

Eliminates Free Radicals

Free radicals are responsible for many illnesses and a lot of the visible signs of aging. These are atoms that cause damage to the cells in our bodies and do nothing but negative things. QiGong can help to reduce and then eliminate free radicals, therefore boosting health and giving you a more youthful look through increased skin elasticity.

Strengthens The Joints And Ligaments

Arthritis sufferers will find great benefit from regular QiGong. By strengthening the joints, pain is reduced, mobility is increased, along with flexibility. This will also cut down on flare-ups and pain over the long-term too.

Speeds up Recovery From Injury

With stronger joints and bones, along with an overall better health picture, you'll find that you recover from injury much faster. All thanks to QiGong! This is particularly useful for athletes and those in training for events.

Boosts Blood Circulation

Any type of exercise or movement that gets your heart rate up a little helps to boost blood circulation, but the more you practice it (more regularly), the better the results. Increased blood flow is ideal for overall health and wellbeing, ensuring that oxygen and nutrients make their way around your body to where they need to be. This can also boost lymphatic drainage, which means that waste is carried out of your body in a timely manner too.

Reduces Stress And Helps With Emotional Balance

The meditation and breathing elements of QiGong are perfect for helping reduce stress. At the start of the book, we talked about the fact that we all have busy lives, and they do nothing but create stress. By practicing QiGong, you'll notice a drastic decrease in stress which will help your physical and mental health.

QiGong can also help you to have a much more pragmatic and balanced view on life, therefore increasing your emotional intelligence. You'll notice that you can balance and control your emotions much easier as a result, with fewer ups and downs than before.

Lower Heart Rate

If you have a high heart rate when you're resting, it's not a good sign. It means that your heart is working harder than it should to be able to pump blood around your body. Of course, your heart rate naturally rises when you're exercising or generally moving around, but when you're resting, a low heart rate is a sign of good health. QiGong can help you to achieve that.

Reduced Muscle Spasms

There are many health problems that can cause painful muscle spasms, such as multiple sclerosis, spinal injury, nervous system problems, anemia, diabetes, thyroid problems, hormone issues, and kidney disease. However, muscle spasms can be reduced with regular QiGong.

Can be Used to Reduce Chronic Pain

All of the benefits we've mentioned above help to create a better picture for anyone who struggles with chronic pain. Regular QiGong provides a gentle and effective way to reduce pain, therefore helping with the quality of life, sleep, and general health and wellbeing. Of course, it also helps with mental health, as nobody will feel their best if they're always struggling with pain and discomfort.

Reduced Blood Pressure

As long as you're eating a healthy diet and you're not indulging in unhealthy habits, such as smoking, regular QiGong could help to reduce your blood pressure. Again, this means there is less stress on your heart, and it boosts your heart health in general while also reducing your risk of stroke.

Helps to Relieve Regular Migraines

Lower stress, increased health, lower anxiety, and better blood flow all help to reduce headaches and migraines. Of course, if you're someone who struggles with regular migraines, you should speak to your doctor and find out the cause, but once that step is out of the way, QiGong may help you to reduce the severity and regularity.

Helps to Improve Posture, Balance, And Flexibility

A little like yoga, QiGong can help to boost flexibility and balance, which goes a long way to improve your posture. Many people have a pretty poor posture and don't even realize it. Slouching and not standing up straight generally can cause back and shoulder pain and can even affect circulation. QiGong can help to rectify that with awareness and the use of poses.

Boosts Immune System Function

A healthy lifestyle helps to boost immune system function, therefore ensuring that you're better protected against illness and you feel better within yourself. However, QiGong includes relaxation, which helps to boost blood flow and the flow of qi, or energy, and helps to regulate breathing levels. All of this creates the perfect storm when it comes to immune system response and can help with the reduction of harmful inflammation within the body.

Helps With Digestion

This is partly down to the posture improvement side of things. When you have a better posture, some digestive issues may decrease or even disappear. However, QiGong also helps to reduce stress, and you will learn how to eat more healthily as part of your new healthier lifestyle. This all helps to reduce digestive issues.

Boosts the Function of The Kidneys

You will remember that when we spoke about yin and yang earlier, we mentioned the kidneys. When you practice regular QiGong, you'll ensure the free flow of qi (energy) throughout the body, and yin and yang will be in balance. This helps to boost kidney function, contributing to the overall health of the body.

Reduced Anxiety & Depression

We should point out that if you are struggling with anxiety and depression, you should go and speak to your doctor. QiGong can help to reduce anxiety and depression, but it may not be suitable for difficult or severe cases. However, overall, regular QiGong can help to relax your mind and allows you to cope with stressful situations. We all know that these types of situations can often be contributors to the development of anxiety and depression to begin with.

QiGong also gives you something you can use to deal with difficult situations, therefore allowing you to cope better with the ups and downs of life.

As you can see, there are many different benefits that QiGong can bring. If this list doesn't convince you, I don't know what will!

Memory Function is Increased

QiGong can help to increase focus, concentration, and memory function. This is the intelligence/scholarly type of QiGong we talked about earlier. Relaxation and meditation can help you to declutter your mind, help you to focus your attention on just one thing, and reduced stress also adds to the benefits. Increased memory function is one of the benefits of QiGong that many people strive toward.

How To Use QiGong For Improving Your Health

You're new to QiGong and only just learning about how it works and what you can do to harness its benefits in your direction. So, you need some tips to help you get started and direct your attention toward boosting your health.

The first thing you need to remember is something we've mentioned already - belief in its power to work. If you don't believe in QiGong, it's not going to work for you. You'll block the energy you're cultivating because of your own negativity. Have an open mind and try it for yourself, but don't doubt it if it doesn't work straight away. It's going to take time before you really notice a difference, but if you're someone who does like to track their progress, why not keep a journal?

This is a healthy habit to have whether you try QiGong or not. Journaling helps you to identify troublesome thoughts and health issues you're facing. Sometimes we're not aware of an actual problem because we're so overloaded with information coming from every direction around us. Journaling helps you to declutter your mind and allows you to focus your attention far better. It can also be a great tool to help boost positive thinking, which is something we all need to work toward doing!

In our next chapter, we're going to delve far deeper into the mechanics of QiGong so you can start to make it work for you, but before that, let's check out some handy tips you can use to increase your chances of QiGong working for your health issues.

The Issue of Imbalances

While health problems occur because of illness or disease in the body, traditional Chinese medicine also believes that everything living gives off an energetic or bioelectric signal/field. When using QiGong, you can work with those signals to help correct imbalances. As a result, you should notice that your health issues have improved.

Imbalances can often build up over many years and come from negative emotions, such as anger, stress, grief, depression, and anxiety, etc.). These are common things we deal with throughout our lives, and, as we've already mentioned, they're far more prevalent in the society today. The imbalances can also be as a result of poor diet (another common issue these days), injury, lack of physical exercise, or indulging in negative habits, such as addiction.

In order to correct these imbalances, the free flow of positive energy throughout the body needs to occur on a regular basis. When blockages occur, that energy cannot move, and it becomes static and stagnant. The parts of the body that aren't receiving the energy suffer, and this can contribute to fatigue, illness, and disease. By using QiGong, you can ensure balance and free flow of energy, in an equal manner throughout.

Don't Rush

It's very easy to start something new and want to keep going at a fast pace. The problem with QiGong is that it's not going to work overnight, as we've already mentioned. But, by pushing your practice too quickly, you're not really developing a strong understanding of your own energy awareness.

You really need to be at one with your body to know when QiGong is starting to work. You need to be totally 'in' your body, and not just in the physical sense. So, in the beginning, it's a good idea to take things steadily and work slowly. Focus on how things feel to you and notice any changes in your awareness or health. We mentioned keeping a journal earlier, and that's a great tool for harnessing your energy awareness skills.

For QiGong to work, you need to be able to awaken your higher consciousnesses. That's not as deep and meaningful as it sounds; it's really about being totally aware of your own existence and how it feels both inside and outside of your body. Meditation will help you to do this, and although that in itself takes practice, you'll notice a calmer and more 'together' feeling over time. That's when you're more aware of your own power, and that's when QiGong will start to work for you.

This is the very basis of QiGong. Without understanding the power of consciousness and how it feels when you start to cultivate energy, you're not going to be able to harness QiGong's power as much as you otherwise would. In that case, you might as well just be doing yoga for the physical health benefits.

Do Not Direct Energy, Let It Build Instead

Many beginners to QiGong think that they already have an abundance of energy, and they simply need to direct it to where it's needed most. The truth is that energy is often zapped daily. Stress and day to day demands all suck the energy out of us and leave us depleted. You've chosen to start using QiGong because you want to cultivate energy and use it to help boost your health and wellbeing. So, the first step shouldn't be to direct energy that you think you already have; it should be to build energy first and then learn how to direct it.

Meditation is often something that people struggle with. It's often assumed that to meditate effectively; you have to quieten your mind completely and not allow even one tiny thought to enter. That's simply unrealistic. The idea isn't to block thoughts. It's to pay no attention to them. By pushing them to one side and focusing your mind, you'll find the meditation becomes easier for you over time. Again, it's not going to be something you master immediately. But, with time, you'll notice progression.

By understanding this concept and not giving up prematurely because you assume that you "can't" meditate, you'll be able to cultivate energy and start grabbing the benefits you seek.

Remember, you were born with qi, or chi, but you can build it up when you focus your attention in the right places.

Posture is Important

Most of us don't naturally have a good posture, as we've already mentioned. Most of us slouch, and that's not helping with back pain or headaches. But, in QiGong, the spine is an important channel for energy. If that channel is blocked because of poor posture, energy isn't able to freely flow up and down and therefore reach all parts of the body.

You can help yourself by being more aware of your posture from the start. Sit up straight - not so that you're uncomfortable, but so that your spine is straight. Also, make sure that your shoulders aren't rounded off, therefore causing a 'block' at the top of your spine. Lift your shoulders up, push them back, and round. That will help your shoulders to remain in alignment with your spine and give you a taller stance.

Practice makes perfect when it comes to improving posture. It's likely that you've picked up some bad habits over your lifetime so far, but know that you can undo them with awareness. By focusing on this, you're already learning how to channel your focus into something, and that's a great start.

Diet is Important Too

A little later, we're going to dedicate a whole section on diet. We know that eating a healthy diet is important for health and wellbeing in general, but when you're a keen follower of QiGong, you need to make sure that you're eating the right things.

This means drinking plenty of water, and cutting out unhealthy and processed foods, including anything with a high sugar content. Eat organic produce as far as possible, and it's also good practice to consume vegetables that are fresh, preferably raw. That way, they still have some life force, or energy, within them, and that can help you to build your own energy stores.

You cannot expect to follow a QiGong lifestyle and eat unhealthily because it's simply not going to bring you the results you want. This needs to be an entire effect in changing your lifestyle. If you want to improve your health and wellbeing, that means looking at what you eat too.

Know What You Want

When you start with anything new, it can be easy to lose momentum and motivation over time. A good way to stop that from happening is if you know what you want to achieve and keep that goal in mind.

What do you want from QiGong? Do you want to feel calmer? Do you want to boost your memory? Do you want to reduce chronic pain? Do you want to boost your fitness level? What is it that you want? Choose one main goal to focus on, because more than that will cause you to feel a little overwhelmed. However, as you achieve one goal, don't be afraid to make more. QiGong is something you can have in your life for many, many years, and that means several goals may come and go.

Some people find it useful to go to classes or find a QiGong practitioner to help them. That's something you can look into, but know that you'll find everything you need to get started in the pages of this book. QiGong is a very personal deal, so you simply need to find the route that works for you.

You could also start QiGong with a friend or family member, but again, it's personal. You can't do QiGong with someone in the same way you can go to a yoga class or a step class together. You're going to be focused and meditative throughout, so it's not really the best situation for talking! But, if having someone beside you motivates you to keep going, then that's perhaps something to look into. It creates accountability, and you can support each other.

Anyone Can Do QiGong

The good news is that you don't need to be extremely fit to start QiGong. It's not something that's going to cause you any struggles if you haven't exercised for a while. As with yoga, there are varying degrees and different poses that you can work up to over time. You will start slowly and move at that pace until you feel that you can step things up a notch. It's a slow process, but one that will bring you benefits.

Anyone can do QiGong, but if you're concerned about anything before you start, don't hesitate to talk to your doctor. That should give you some reassurance and the confidence to get started.

You also don't need any props or equipment to start QiGong. You already have everything you need - your body and your mind. You can also do QiGong anywhere that feels comfortable to you, but it's always going to boost your efforts if you go somewhere quiet and natural. A field, near the sea, a mountain, anywhere with a good view, your garden even. These are all fantastic spots to focus on QiGong because Mother Nature will do her bit to help you out with focus and concentration.

If you struggle with any of the poses, you can use the wall, a tree, or even a chair for support. Over time, you may find that you no longer need to use support, but if you do, that's fine too.

There is no evidence to suggest that QiGong has any side effects but remember that changing your lifestyle is a large thing, so as before, talk to your doctor if you have any concerns, especially in relation to diet. When doing any of the poses, know that at first, they may cause you to feel a little unbalanced, especially if you have poor balance to begin with. In that case, use something for support, to avoid the risk of falling over and injuring yourself.

The good news is that QiGong uses slow and controlled movements, so the chances of injury or falls are very low indeed.

Find Support And Advice

There are a lot of resources out there for help if you feel like you want to ask questions or you need clarification on something. The Internet is a fantastic place to find help on QiGong. You can reach out to a social media group who are all about QiGong, or you can find a practitioner or teacher to seek advice from.

Don't feel that QiGong has to be something done in solitude all the time. Yes, it's for you and you alone, but there are people out there to help if you need help or advice. It's better to reach out than to give up completely, as most issues can be solved very easily with a different viewpoint or a simple piece of advice to take on board.

What Are The Main Differences Between Tai Chi And QiGong?

At the very start of the book, we mentioned that QiGong and Tai Chi are different. It's important to know why because it's easy to become confused between the two if you're not totally sure.

You need to focus your mind on the cultivation of energy, and then, your body and higher spirit will do the job of moving the energy around your body, to the places that need it the most. You won't be able to do that if you're confused in any way.

Tai chi is about movement, just as Tai Chi, but it's not about cultivating energy as QiGong is. Tai chi was originally developed to help with martial arts training, but these days it's used for health. You'll find all different age groups making use of this practice, and to great effect.

Tai chi is sometimes known as a form of mobile or moving meditation. It involves motions that are quite gentle, and they take their form from natural movements. Tai chi movements happen mostly while standing upright and using very small steps.

You can see how people would be a little confused between the two, but QiGong is different.

QiGong is about energy. It's not solely about movements, and there's a lot more to it. It's about meditation, visualization, movement, and breathing. It's also about diet and a healthy lifestyle. If Tai Chi is more physical, you could say that QiGong is more inward; it's about the internal processes, not solely about the external.

QiGong poses are stationary poses - you don't move. You simply repeat the poses a set number of times, depending upon the pose and the targeted need. Then, you think about how you feel, becoming more aware of your body and your higher self.

So, now can you see the differences?

They're subtle, but they're there.

Tai chi is a series of movements that flow from one to another. QiGong is a movement that is designed for a specific situation. The pose is repeated until the benefit is felt. Tai chi moves all the time. QiGong doesn't.

For sure, they both bring major benefits, and some of them overlap, but QiGong is about a more rounded experience than Tai Chi.

Points to Remember

This chapter should have achieved its aim - to convince you that QiGong is a positive and very worthwhile endeavor to start. It will help you to push aside any negative thoughts you have about the practice and look forward to what it can bring to you.

For sure, it's not going to happen overnight, but nothing good ever comes without a little work, right? In this case, you'll enjoy what you're doing, and you'll see results. At the same time, you'll feel in control of your life and, most importantly, in control of your health.

The most important points to take from this chapter are:

- QiGong has many benefits for health and wellbeing
- The benefits encompass physical, mental, emotional, and spiritual health
- You need to start slowly and understand that benefits won't come to you overnight
- Journaling is a great way to build awareness and log your progress
- Understanding your 'why' helps you to focus on the benefits you want to achieve
- If you don't believe in QiGong, it's not going to work for you - push aside those negative thoughts!
- Imbalances in the body lead to illness and disease. QiGong helps to unblock and get the energy flowing, therefore improving your health
- A life of negativity, poor habits, stress, anxiety, and other negative emotions can cause energy to be blocked. QiGong can unblock it
- You need to have a strong consciousness within your own body and understand your own power
- Focus on energy awareness and understanding when you're building and cultivating energy, rather than looking for instant results
- Focus on building energy at the start and not simply directing it
- You need to look at your diet if you want QiGong to work - eat foods that are fresh and raw as far as possible

- Poor posture can block energy - stand up straight!
- Anyone can do QiGong, but if you have any concerns, speak to your doctor first
- You can use support during the poses if you need to - you won't harm your energy cultivation by doing this
- Help and support are out there if you need it, but QiGong is a personal endeavor
- QiGong is different from Tai Chi.
- Understand what you want to achieve and keep a goal in mind for motivation

Chapter 3:
The Critical Phases Of Qi Cultivation

QiGong isn't easy to understand at the start, but by this point, you should have a lot more information than you did before. That should help you to start feeling more confident about what's to come.

In this chapter, we're going to focus more on the three components that make up QiGong. For sure, we've said 'poses,' but what poses? How do they work? How long do you hold them for? All will be revealed!

We're also going to talk about meditation, breathing, and visualization a bit more and give you confidence that it will work for you.

It may seem like a lot to take on board right now, but you've learned a lot so far. You can go back and re-read any parts that aren't clear to you at any time - we're going to be your guide through the world of QiGong, so don't be worried about not grasping everything at the first turn - few people do!

By showing a real interest in making QiGong work for you, the benefits will be greater. So, ask questions, go back over things, highlight parts if you need to and then learn more! The point is that it's a process you need to absorb, and then the good stuff can begin.

Understanding The Principles Behind QiGong May Be Challenging

For many, understanding how QiGong works can be difficult. As we've already mentioned, it's important to put any preconceived notions to one side, but it's also worthwhile digging into the ins and outs a little more. Before we go into the components in more detail, let's run through a few other points deeply.

You may be wondering what happens to your body when you're using breathing exercises and imagery, or what happens when you're practicing a posture. It's not easy to give a definite answer to that because everyone's body alignments are different. You may be blocked in one specific area, not allowing energy to flow quite so freely, but your friend may have a blockage or a misalignment somewhere else. But, the basic explanation is that the three main components of QiGong help energy to flow more freely.

But, how exactly?

The whole idea of QiGong is based upon energy. This energy is very subtle and can't be seen or felt, but it is very powerful. Chinese philosophy states that the build up of energy helps with the manifestation of the physical form, i.e., your actual body. This is done with the help of qi, jing, and Shen.

What are these?

Let's talk about these in turn.

Shen is related to the mind and spirit, and when energy reaches the correct level, it helps with consciousness and form. However, when Shen is misaligned, disturbances can occur, such as mental illness and negative thinking.

Qi, as we already know, is an important energy that flows through the body and helps to ensure the smooth running of the body and the function of the organs. When qi is flowing freely, you'll feel healthy, you'll have more energy, and you'll notice a lighter feeling within yourself.

And finally, we have jing. This is a physical energy that is associated with vitality and sexual function. All three elements come together to ensure overall health and wellbeing. But, before that point, all three help to manifest the spiritual, emotional, and physical elements of a person. You can't have one without the other; they all work together to support the others.

Traditional Chinese medicine is based upon this idea, and many different practices use the philosophy, including acupuncture and medicine massage. QiGong is also based upon this philosophy with the use of the three main components - breath, visualization, and movement.

Each component has an effect in its own right, but when they're used together, the effects are amplified, and the results are far more positive.

Let's take a look at the three components in turn before we finally move on to the practical elements of how to use them.

The Role Of Breath In QiGong

Breath is the one thing you have with you throughout your entire life. You're born with breath, and it's with you until the day you die - the day you take your final breath. However, breath changes according to our emotions and situations.

When you're panicked and stressed, you breathe in a shallow manner, from the top of the chest. However, when you're calm and centered, you breathe from the abdomen in a more controlled and slow way. When you're practicing QiGong, you will use a specific pattern of breathing - in through the nose deeply and out through the mouth for a slightly longer time. The idea is that this pattern helps you to breathe out a greater amount of carbon dioxide, therefore allowing more space for life-giving oxygen to enter the body.

In traditional Chinese medicine, the lungs are vitally important because not only do they allow you to breathe, but they help to regulate energy. As you breathe in and out, the lungs help to move qi (energy) around your body, pushing it down into the lower parts and giving your vital organs what they need to work in the most effective way possible. The lungs are also responsible for guarding the skin's surface, therefore providing a protein barrier against external threats that could enter through the skin's top layer.

Breathing exercises help to make the most of your breath and ensure that it makes its way around your body as much as possible, but it's about more than that. Breath is very strongly related to relaxation and spirituality. Many spiritual traditions use breath and meditation to connect with a higher power or with their own higher version of themselves. Breath, when used correctly, can help you to become more aware of yourself and how you feel.

Of course, from a medical point of view, breath is vital for life. Without it, you die.

Different types of breathing have different effects on the body. For instance, abdominal diaphragmatic breathing (breathing from just above the navel) helps to bring down blood pressure and send oxygenated blood around the body in a more effective way - boosting oxygen levels in the blood itself. This type of breathing is important because it also helps to pull qi down to the bottom half of the body while helping to relax and concentrate the mind.

There is another type of breathing used in QiGong, called focused lower belly breathing. This helps to protect the lungs, spleen, digestive system, and the kidneys. Yet, active breathing, the type that we tend to do when we're stressed, can also be used to good effect in the right situation. It will increase blood pressure a little, but it can also add stimulation to the lungs and heart and can help to move qi around the body in a stronger and faster way. These aren't the only types of breathing you can use in QiGong.

We're going to talk later on about the different types of breathing and how to use them, but for now, know that breath is a vital part of

39

the entire practice, and manipulating your breath in specific breathing exercises can help you to target parts of your body and receive the benefits you're looking for.

QiGong and Body Postures

We've already talked about the fact that poor posture is rife in modern society and that it can drastically affect the flow of qi around the body. In QiGong, however, postures are used to change consciousness and manipulate the flow of qi through the body.

The importance of posture comes from the spine. This is a vital energy channel, and when there is a small kink or blockage of any type, it stops energy from flowing freely. Of course, the spine has many functions, and it's a main communication channel from the brain to the main organs, while also giving support to help with standing and movement.

The position of the spine also affects how the main organs function and how they work together for optimum health and wellbeing. A poor posture can compress the organs and can stop blood, oxygen, and qi from flowing. It can also affect the digestive system, resulting in many unpleasant symptoms.

Compression of the spine and internal organs can also cause old or stagnant blood to build up, along with waste products from cells. This causes the blood to have less oxygen within it, and as a result, it's unable to absorb energy and oxygen from the lungs, or move it around the body.

It's not just the spine, it's the extremities that are linked to it too. For instance, the wrists, fingers, shoulders, and elbows are also connected to the main organs, including the heart, lungs, pericardium, and intestines. Injury or problems in these areas can affect the flow of energy to these organs while also causing muscle tension.

In QiGong, postures are practiced until the desired benefits are achieved. You don't move through a series of postures as you would in yoga or Tai Chi. In this case, you will focus until you achieve. The idea is that you are conscious of your choice, and when you're in the posture, you're consciously focusing upon it. As a result, the problems you want to improve are affected.

However, there are exercises that use repetitive movements. These are used to help boost qi flow, specifically in the nervous system and circulation. Using these repetitive types of movement also helps to free up blockages and allows qi to flow freely once more.

The other plus point of these movements is that the contraction and relaxation of the muscles help to push oxygen and nutrients through the capillaries while also helping to flush toxins and waste out of the body.

When you slow your movements down, the nervous system is affected, therefore helping with the digestive system, respiratory system, urinary system, and the reproductive system.

There are many different postures and movements to use in QiGong, and it depends upon your aims as to which ones you will choose. While it may seem challenging at the moment, we're going to talk about some important exercises in the coming chapter, giving you something to start off with.

The Underestimated Power Of Visualization

The third component of QiGong is visualization and meditation. These two are often grouped together because they're so closely linked, and one often leads to the other.

You might misinterpret the idea of visualization. You're not actually looking to see something with your eyes; instead, you're picturing it in your mind's eye. In effect, you're using your imagination. If you were famed for your vivid imagination when you were younger, it's going to come in very handy now!

Yet, visualization is about more than seeing something in your mind. You have to be so into the picture you're creating that you feel it. You need to become aware of the energy flowing throughout your mind and body when visualizing, to help push forward your efforts.

If you simply see the picture and don't feel it or really push yourself into the picture, you're simply daydreaming.

Visualization shouldn't be stressful, and it shouldn't make you feel tense either. If you feel tense, energy is blocked. When you're allowing thoughts to constantly flow into your mind, you're not going to be able to submit to your visualization exercise. In this case, you need to use relaxation and allow the zen part of your mind to take over. How? By using meditation.

That's why the two often work hand in hand. By practicing meditation, you'll find your visualization efforts are much stronger and the benefits far better as a result. Again, we're going to run through some exercises you can try later on.

Being able to relax and visualize helps with the flow of qi. A tense body causes blockages and misalignment, totally going against what we're trying to achieve. Being able to relax is also extremely beneficial for mental health and relaxation. By understanding how to deeply relax your mind and body, through meditation and the use of visualization, you're not only ensuring the free flow of energy, but you're also improving the quality of your life through less stress and reduced anxiety.

Of course, meditation and visualization are also associated with the ability to be able to concentrate. In traditional Chinese medicine, this is closely linked to Shen, the type of energy we talked about earlier. Shen is about the mind and spirituality. As you learn how to concentrate and focus your mind, you're increasing Shen energy.

Points to Remember

Understanding how QiGong works and how you end up with the benefits you're aiming toward can be confusing. Remember, this is all very new to you right now, and nobody expects you to understand everything immediately. Traditional Chinese medicine can be a mystery from the outside, but as you learn, experience, and explore, you start to understand its nuances in greater detail.

So, if you're struggling to really pinpoint in your mind what's going on, or you have a grasp on it now, but you have to really focus on keeping your mind on track, don't worry. That's exactly where you need to be right now. What you're embarking upon isn't a new hobby. It's a complete lifestyle overhaul. These things take time.

The main points to remember from this chapter are:

- QiGong helps to boost the free flow of energy (qi) around the body
- Qi, Jing, and Shen are different types of essences or energies that create the manifesto of your physical, mental, and spiritual sides
- The lungs are very important in QiGong as they help to distribute qi, oxygen, and nutrients throughout the body, particularly down to the lower half of the body
- Traditional Chinese medicine is based upon the ideas of these three essences, all of which work together to ensure health, balance, and harmony
- In QiGong, you will hold postures and focus on them until you notice a difference in your symptoms or benefits come your way

- The use of breath in QiGong is very important. There are different types of breathing you can do to help with specific problems
- However, there are slow and repeated movements also involved, which help to boost the flow of qi that may have become static or stagnated
- Visualization is the third element of QiGong, and this works hand in hand with meditation and relaxation
- Visualization isn't just about seeing something in your mind; it's about feeling it and really being 'in' the image
- Learning to relax has countless benefits and can help with the manifestation of Shen.

Chapter 4:
Best QiGong Exercises You Need to Practice

Now it's time to get practical!

You know the basics of QiGong, and you're keen to get started. That's the spirit!

The different postures and movements associated with QiGong vary according to your desired outcome. You don't have to follow the examples we've given in this chapter, but these exercises are designed to help you understand the most important postures and movements for beginners. From there, you can research and learn new postures and movements that will help you to achieve your aims.

We know that QiGong uses breathing, visualization, meditation, and physical movement to increase and boost the flow of energy. QiGong is also designed to allow you to boost your Jing and Shen.

When working with these exercises, remember the yin and yang we talked about earlier. Yin is the actual thing, i.e., being the thing. Yang is actually taking action and doing it. Keeping all of this in mind during your exercises will help you to boost your energy.

Let's Get Started With Three Efficient Warm-up Exercises

Before you start with your exercises, you need to warm up. This is the same as any other type of physical movement. You wouldn't go in with cold muscles, and the same thing applies here. So, before we get into some actual postures and movements to try, let's look at three specific warm-up exercises you can begin with.

You can use all three, find one that suits you best, or alternate them according to how you feel.

Gentle Sway

The first exercise is called the 'Gentle Sway' and should be done for 5 minutes.

- Stand with your legs slightly apart and your arms hanging down by your sides
- Move your arms, making sure that you move them from your shoulder in a swinging movement
- As you move, twist lightly from the waist, not the knees. This part will massage your internal organs
- Then, move your arms in a side to side motion across your body
- Alternate the direction of your arm movements, remembering to keep your knees bent very slightly
- Clear your mind and don't pay any attention to any thoughts that enter your mind
- Try and focus on building energy by moving your arms, but don't worry if this is difficult at first.

The Posture of Infinity

The posture of infinity is a good way to help develop a better posture. It makes you more aware of how you're standing and the tension you may be holding. This movement can be done for up to 5 minutes, but again, start with less time and work up.

- Stand with your legs a shoulder-width apart, your knees slightly bent, and your eyes looking straight ahead
- Keep your chin tucked under and keep your arms and shoulders relaxed
- Take a breath and focus on your posture, becoming aware of any tension you feel

- You should be able to stand upright without feeling any muscular tension or pain
- Hold the posture.

The Bounce

The bounce can be done for 3 minutes, although start at 1 minute and work up.

- Stand with your legs a shoulder-width apart, with your knees bent very slightly and your arms hanging loosely by your side. Keep your arms loose and avoid any tension
- Don't hold any tension in your shoulders; allow them to roll forward if that feels natural to you
- Notice how your body feels relaxed
- When you're ready, slowly and gently start to bounce, using your feet
- The movement helps to massage the organs and keeps your mind in the moment. Again, if any thoughts enter your mind, ignore them and focus on the building of energy.

Powerful QiGong Exercises You Have To Try

After you've warmed up, it's time to start with some QiGong exercises. Now, remember there are many different exercises out there, and it's simply not possible to list them all. You should start with the basics and then work up as you feel more confident.

Within this section, we're also going to talk about a series of movements that are called the Eight Pieces of Brocade. This obviously consists of eight different poses and is one of the most important series of poses in QiGong. However, these can be used independently as you see fit and don't necessarily need to be followed in order once you get used to them.

The Accordion

If you picture the movement you will make when playing the accordion, you can appreciate the type of movement you're going to make here as you boost qi flow and cultivate more energy. This exercise is ideal for beginners as it helps you to become aware of what energy feels like.

- Close your eyes and open them ever so slightly to a half-lidded position
- Keep your mind as clear as possible and focus your attention on the palms of your hands
- Allow your breathing to become slow and gentle. You should feel totally relaxed
- When you're ready, bring your palms together in front of you, ensuring that your fingers point up to the ceiling. Make sure that the center of your palms are touching one another. There are important chakras in the palms, and these will help to generate qi
- Move your hands apart very slowly, keeping your palms in alignment so that the chakras remain connected. Move your hands by no more than 30cm and then slowly move them back together again
- You should feel a warm sensation and a slight resistance from the air between your hands
- Continue the same movement, and if you want to change direction, e.g., up and down, you can do that too.

Extending The Qi

This is another good exercise for beginners. When you first start with QiGong, it's likely that you don't have enough energy, or you have a blockage or misalignment. This exercise will help you to get qi moving. There are two ways to do this exercise - with your eyes half-lidded or completely open. If you feel like you are lacking in qi, keep your eyes half-lidded. If you feel like you have energy, but it's not moving well, you can keep your eyes open. If you're not sure, play around with both options and see which feels right to you.

- Stand with your legs very slightly apart, with your body relaxed
- Breathe in quickly through your nose and focus on the energy in your body
- Visualize the energy moving through your body and out. As you breathe in, picture it moving in and as you breathe out, picture it expanding outward. This is your orbit
- Continue with this visualization as you breathe, trying to push the orbit a little further with every exhalation
- If it helps, use your arms to assist in the visualization, moving them up and down as you breathe.

The Eight Pieces of Brocade

The Eight Pieces of Brocade is a very important series of movements in QiGong. As we mentioned before, you can do these in a series as you feel confident, or you can use them independently. However, remember that QiGong is not the same as Tai Chi, so you shouldn't allow them to blend from one to another.

To get the best results from these poses, you need to relax as much as you can. Each movement will be done with your feet flat on the floor, with slightly bent knees. You shouldn't feel any tension in your body. Make sure that you breathe slowly and don't hold your breath at any point - it's very easy to do that when you're trying to concentrate on something new, but you'll block the flow of energy by doing that. Keep breathing!

Each movement should be repeated eight times, but if you struggle at first, you can do fewer repetitions until you feel more confident. As you do the movements, place your tongue on the top of your mouth, keeping it behind your teeth. This should be a light touch and not a firm press. As you're moving, make sure that you move very slowly and gently. Focus on the growth of energy around you and the movement.

Now, let's look at each individual one of the eight pieces.

Pushing Up The Heavens

The first of the Eight Pieces of Brocade is Pushing Up The Heavens. This movement is designed to focus on the lungs, heart, spleen, and stomach. It is also focused on the kidneys and liver too, so it's a great choice for anyone who wants to help with general health and wellbeing. In addition to all of this, this exercise is also known to relax the body, and lower blood pressure and heart rate, while also boosting blood circulation.

- Stand with your legs slightly apart, and your hands should be positioned so that your palms are facing inward, toward your legs
- Breathe in, and on the exhale, move your palms up, so they're facing outward
- Keep moving your palms up until they reach the same level as your chest/heart. At that point, turn your palms, so they face outward
- Exhale as you push your hands further upward
- As you breathe in, move your hands back down
- The exhale should begin as your hands reach chest/heart level once more, until they're back down to your sides.

Pulling The Bow to Shoot the Arrow

The second move is ideal for boosting your kidneys and lungs. We've already talked at length about the importance of the lungs in QiGong, so this is a good all-rounder exercise to go for. This particular exercise is also important for the muscles, including the knees, legs, and abdominals. If you struggle with back pain due to muscular tension, this is a good option for soothing that pain.

- Stand with your legs a little more than a shoulder-width apart and bend your knees a little more than in the other exercise
- Take a breath in as you cross your arms over your body
- Exhale as you pull back as though you're shooting an arrow
- On the next inhale, cross your arms again, and on the exhale, pull back with the other arm in the same movement
- On the final inhale, cross your arms once more and then exhale, returning your arms back to your sides.

Separating Heaven And Earth

The third movement is aimed at helping the spleen and stomach. It's also known to be useful for muscular aches and pains while also boosting circulation.

- Stand with your legs a shoulder-width apart and keep your arms down by your sides, with your palms facing your legs
- As you breathe in, cross your arms in line with your chest
- As you breathe out, slowly raise one arm upwards and move the other downwards. Keep your arms slightly bent for comfort
- As you inhale once more, switch the arms, so the one that was facing up is now facing down and vice versa
- As you exhale, move the arms in the opposite direction once more
- On your final inhalation, bring your arms back down to a neutral position, by your sides with your palms facing your legs.

The Wise Owl Gaze Backward

If you picture the stance of an owl, you'll be able to imagine this movement in your mind. This movement is ideal for helping with circulation, particularly two very important blood vessels in the front and back of your body. It also helps with deep relaxation as well as improving posture by lengthening and straightening the spine.

- As with the other movements, start with your legs a shoulder-width apart and your arms by your sides. The difference here is that your palms need to face up, and you need to bend your knees a little
- As you breathe out, push your hands down and straighten your legs. Make sure that as you do this, you picture your spine straightening out and energy flowing freely
- As you straighten, open your hands so that your fingers spread and push your arms out as far as they will go
- Turn to look behind your left shoulder for 5 seconds
- Take a deep breath in and repeat the movement again, but this time turning to look over your right shoulder
- On your final inhalation, turn your head to face the front once more and return to the original position, with your palms facing upward
- As you exhale, your arms should slowly move back to your sides.

Swaying The Head And Swinging The Tail

The next movement is designed to boost lung function, benefit the kidneys and heart, and helps with anxiety and worry. It can also be useful for anyone with lower back pain, knee issues, and any leg problems. This is another good move for anyone with poor posture, as it helps to boost spine mobility.

- Stand with your legs wide apart and bend your knees
- Rest your hands on your thighs
- Breathe in and as you exhale move your body to the right in a swaying motion and turn diagonally so that your nose is in a straight line with the big toe on your left foot
- Take a breath in and move to the opposite side, breathing out as you move across your body
- When you have finished this movement, return to center on an inhale and slowly stand up straight
- Exhale as your hands move back to your sides.

Two Hands Hold The Feet to Strengthen The Kidneys

This particular movement is designed to boost the function of the kidneys while also being a beneficial option for anyone with lower back problems and leg pain. It is specifically good for the hamstrings and abdominal muscles. As such, it is a good movement for strengthening the core and correcting poor posture.

- Stand with your legs wide apart and a very slight bend in your knees for comfort
- Take your hands and hold them in front of your navel, creating a 'frame' shape over your navel with your fingers
- Take a breath in and move your hands slowly around your waist to your lower back
- On the exhale, bend forward very slightly while slowly moving your hands to the backs of your legs. Continue moving down slowly until your hands are touching your heels
- Hold that position for 3 seconds
- As you breathe in again, move your hands slowly back up your legs and move back into your starting position, with your hands framing your naval
- On the final repetition, exhale and move your hands back down to your sides.

Punching With Angry Eyes

The punching motion used in this seventh piece is designed to increase your abdominal power and boost liver function. It's also a good option for anyone who is holding anger or grudges against other people. This can help you to release such negative emotions and move on. For anyone who has leg muscle problems, this is also a useful movement to try as it is known to strengthen the leg muscles.

- Stand with your legs wide apart and bend deeply in your knees
- With your hands by your sides, clench your fists slightly, not holding too much tension in the hands
- Focus your eyes forward and imagine fire and anger - your face should mirror this and should take on an angry expression
- Take a breath in and when you breathe out, punch forward with your left hand, making sure that you keep the movement slow and controlled. Your fist should twist around so that your clenched hand is facing the floor
- Take a breath in and move your hand back down to your side. The palm of your fisted hand should face up
- Exhale and repeat the movement with your other hand
- On the last repetition, inhale as you slowly stand upright, with your hands relaxed and returned to your sides.

Bouncing on Heels to Shake Off Stress And Illness

The final of the eight movements that make up the Brocade is designed to boost the immune system and help you to push aside any stress or lingering feelings of negativity. It's also a great choice for anyone who has a problem with their feet or calves. This movement will make you feel energized and is also said to clear the mind.

- Stand with your legs straight and your heels touching one another, creating a V shape
- Your hands should be by your sides with your palms facing inwards, towards your legs
- On your inhale, move your hands up with your palms facing upward, bending your knees a little as you do so
- On your exhale, turn your palms to face downward and push your arms down, straightening your legs as you do so
- Move onto your tiptoes and hold the position for 3 seconds, continuing to exhale

- Then, bounce slowly on your heels, allowing your body to move naturally, without any force
- You should repeat this eight times and on the final round, return your feet to a flat position
- Shake your body eight times, moving your knees and arms how you please.

Remember, there are many movements associated with QiGong, and we don't have the time or the space to write them all down for you! But, these are some of the basic and most important movements you should master before attempting to move on with your QiGong practice.

Take your time and really feel each movement. Remember to visualize energy being created and flowing freely throughout your body as you move slowly.

It's possible that some movements simply won't feel natural to you or simply won't work for you. That's fine. Everyone is different, there is no 'one size fits all' answer to anything - QiGong included. But, you should at least give them a good try and don't give up too soon. If, after a while, it's simply not doing anything for you, you can move on to another movement and try that instead. You will certainly find a series of movements that give you the results you're looking for. Sometimes it's simply a case of trial and error.

Points to Remember

This has been our first real practical chapter, and we've given you a series of movements to try when getting started on your QiGong journey. We've also given you three warm-up exercises too.

It's important to remember that the first or second time you try these exercises, it's going to feel strange; you may feel everything or nothing. You may feel something you're not sure about. All of this is very normal. QiGong takes time to master, and it's a journey that is worth the effort. Even seasoned QiGong practitioners go through times when they can't quite connect with their inner energy, so as a beginner, it's to be expected for you too.

The main points to remember from this chapter are:

- There are many QiGong exercises to try, but you should focus on a few, to begin with, and try to master those before moving on to more advanced exercises
- Remember that QiGong isn't the same as Tai Chi. You don't move through a series of poses in the same way. Instead, you focus on exercises that are beneficial to you and stick with them until you feel the benefits
- There isn't a 'one size fits all 'approach to QiGong. There are guidelines and advice, but you should tailor your practice to your own needs and goals
- Remember to persevere and don't give up too soon - you're not going to see results overnight, but they will come eventually
- If an exercise simply isn't working for you after a little time, or it just doesn't feel right, that's fine. Not every exercise works for everyone.

Chapter 5:
Highly Powerful Breathing Techniques

We've talked about exercises and movements to get started, but none of that will work well without breath.

You'll remember that in the exercises, we simply talked about inhaling and exhaling, but is it that simple? Not if you want to get the most out of your QiGong practice, no.

In this chapter, we will talk about, other than the obvious, why breathing is so important. We'll then explain how you can use your breath as an anchor during difficult times and how it can help you to absorb more energy, or qi. Then, we're going to give you some practice breathing exercises to try.

Why is Breath So Important?

We need to breathe to stay alive. That's the basics and the thing we all know. When we stop breathing, things aren't going so well, to say the least. It's true that your breath is the only thing in your life that will be with you from the day you're born until the day you finally leave this life. It's something you can use to help cope with difficult situations and manipulate how you feel, and it's also a way to absorb more qi, or energy.

Breathing obviously helps you to take in oxygen, which is then carried around the body. But what else? Breathing is used to balance out the heart rate and help you to feel calmer and sharper. It's also a way to become more energized, boost the immune system, and help you deal with stress on a day-to-day basis.

From a QiGong point of view, breath is known as the "rhythm of life." It's an even and constant series of movements that don't stop. The basic pattern in QiGong breathing is something that most of us don't do, but with practice, this will become your go-to route.

Rather than simply breathing in and out through your nose, or even worse, through your mouth, you need to alternate this. Breathe in deeply through the nose and then exhale for a longer time through the mouth.

There are several benefits to this pattern. Firstly, it's calming and grounding, but it also helps to release carbon dioxide and makes space in the lungs for nourishing oxygen. Of course, with that oxygen comes qi.

You cannot practice QiGong without being able to focus on your breathing and use it hand in hand with visualization. We're going to talk about specific visualization exercises and how to do them later on, but it's a good option to try alongside breathing exercises.

Your breath is something that will help you endlessly when you're trying to master meditation. If you find that your mind wanders, as it will at the start, you can turn your attention to your breath and center yourself once more. If you find that you're becoming angry in your day-to-day life, focus on your breath, and you'll calm down pretty quickly. If you can't concentrate, focus on your breath, and your mind will reset.

Put simply, your breath is so much more than lungs expanding and deflating. It's a vital process that not only keeps you alive but also keeps you focused and healthy.

Breath As An Anchor

We just mentioned the fact that your breathing can be something you use in difficult situations. Let's delve into that a little more because it may be something you're missing out on in your day-to-day life.

When we become upset or stressed, we breathe differently. If you've ever experienced the terrifying process of a panic attack, you probably felt like you couldn't breathe, or you couldn't get enough oxygen into your lungs fast enough. In truth, nothing was actually going to harm you in that moment; it's simply that you were breathing in from your chest in a shallow way that wouldn't allow you to take in the oxygen you needed to control your breath and calm down. That is why when people experience panic attacks, they're often advised to breathe into a paper bag - it turns their awareness to the breath, and they can picture the bag expanding and deflating. That's all it takes to affect breathing patterns and calm the situation down.

That's how powerful breath can be.

Breathing from the chest means that you can't expand your lungs fast enough, and you feel short of breath. That kickstarts the panic reaction and causes you to either feel like you're having a panic attack or causes a stress reaction. By being more aware of the breath and breathing from the right place, e.g., the abdomen, you'll be able to take in as much oxygen as you need and focus on calming your thoughts and emotions.

There's a reason why people say "take a few deep breaths" when someone is angry. Breathing is connected very closely to emotions, and a few minutes of calm, focused breathing can be enough to take someone out of a heightened state of emotion and get them to calm down. When you add visualization to the mix, the results are even more positive.

If you've ever tried yoga, you'll also understand that breath is key. The same goes for QiGong. It's a way to focus your mind, but it's also hugely important in terms of taking in qi and allowing it to move freely around the body.

If you're ever struggling with negative emotions or you're in a situation where you feel like you want to move out of that headspace for a moment, sit and close your eyes and then focus on your breath. Try the circular breathing technique we mentioned in the first section of this chapter, and picture your stomach expanding and deflating as you do. You'll notice that after a few seconds or a minute or two, you feel much calmer and more clear-headed. It's a grounding tool that you always have at your disposal; you just need to learn how to use it properly.

Breath Will Help You Absorb Qi

By this point, you'll be very clear on the fact that QiGong is the cultivation and flow of qi, or energy, around the body. We know that this happens through poses/movements, visualization and meditation, and breathing. But, how can breath help you to absorb more qi and therefore boost your efforts?

Breath is an ever-present thing anyway. But, by manipulating your breath and using visualization as much as possible, you can help to manifest and absorb more qi.

Qi is all around you, but negative thinking and problems with the chakras within the body stop qi from getting into your body and moving around freely. Breath helps to free up those blockages, and along with movements and visualization, allows more qi to do its job.

When you inhale, you breathe in qi. When you exhale, you breathe out stagnant energy or negativity. The more you do it, the more negativity and stagnant energy you get rid of and the more new energy you take in.

It's really that simple.

Evidence of the importance of breath in QiGong and other traditional Chinese medicine methods dates back as far as the 6th century BCE. It was Lao Tzu who was the first to talk about how breathing can be used to cultivate and boost qi. From there, two specific breathing methods were talked about. These include Buddha's breathing and Daoist's breathing.

These are known to help take in as much qi from the environment as possible and can also be very good focus methods when using meditation for the first time.

Many QiGong breathing exercises are based upon these two specific breathing types. Let's take a look at them in more detail.

Buddha's Breath

Buddha's breath got its name for several reasons. Firstly, Buddha and meditation go hand in hand, and this type of breathing is a great meditation tool. Secondly, it's also about the posture you take when breathing in this manner.

We mentioned earlier about not breathing from your chest. That simply restricts lung capacity and doesn't allow you to take in as much qi as you could otherwise absorb. Instead, you need to focus on breathing from your abdomen. If you put your hand over your navel and just below, that's basically where you need to breathe from. For the first few times, put your hand there and feel the expansion and deflation; that will help you to focus on breathing from the right place.

When using this exercise, indeed any breathing exercise, make sure that your spine is straight. You can either lay down flat, sit up straight, or stand up. The choice is yours, but your spine needs to be straight so that the flow of qi isn't interrupted.

To do Buddha breathing:

- Inhale and feel your abdomen extending outwards as it absorbs oxygen and qi. Inhale for a count of eight
- Exhale for a count of sixteen and, as you do so, contract your abdominal muscles (also known as your core) to push the air slowly and steadily out from the bottom of the lungs, through your mouth. As you exhale, your abdomen will deflate
- While you're inhaling and exhaling, imagine qi flowing into your body and nourishing your organs.

Buddha breathing is perhaps the most natural of the two types. You'll quickly see from our next type (Daoist breathing) that you'll probably need to concentrate a little more to get the movement right. For that reason, start with Buddha breathing first and master that before moving on to the next type.

Daoist Breathing

The second type that forms the basis for QiGong is called Daoist breathing. This is very similar to Buddha breathing, except you do the opposite. As with Buddha breathing, you need to make sure that you focus your attention completely on the process of inhaling and exhaling while imagining qi flowing into your body. Without the visualization aspect, you're simply not going to get the benefit.

To try Daoist breathing:

- Again, make sure that your spine is straight before you begin
- Place your hands over your abdomen to help you focus
- Inhale through your nose for a count of eight, but this time you need to contract your abdominal muscles and pull them in on the inhale

- Exhale for a count of sixteen, relaxing your abdominal muscles and feeling them push outward as the breath pushes out of your lungs and eventually out of your mouth

It's very possible that you will feel more comfortable doing either Buddha breathing or Daoist breathing. One will feel natural to you, and the other may feel more forced - that's normal. However, many people don't naturally breathe from their abdomen, so before we move on to the breathing exercises to try, practice abdominal breathing first and foremost. Then, you'll get more benefit from the exercises we're about to talk you through.

If you do regularly breathe from your chest, usually in a shallow manner, that's usually a sign of stress or anxiety. By redirecting your breath down to your abdomen, you'll increase your lung capacity and be able to take in more oxygen and qi regularly. That in itself will allow you to feel calmer and more grounded.

QiGong Breathing Exercises You Can Start With

You now understand how important breath is, far more than just keeping you alive. In this section, we're going to give you some practical breathing techniques to try. As with the movements we talked about in our last chapter, it's possible that some will come easier to you than others.

The difference between the movement exercises and the breathing exercises is that anyone can master the breathing techniques. It simply takes time and practice. It's normal for some to feel more natural to you than others, but that doesn't mean you won't be able to master it in a short amount of time.

The more breathing techniques you have at your disposal, the more you'll be able to absorb qi and benefit from its nourishing and uplifting effects.

In this section, we're going to talk about:

- Cleansing breathing
- Original breathing
- Tortoise breathing
- Kidney breathing
- Embryonic breathing
- Reverse breathing

These are some of the easiest breathing methods to start with as a QiGong enthusiast, and they're also very beneficial from the get-go. You don't have to work through them in order; you can simply choose the one that suits you best and start with that, but it's always a good idea to practice the Buddha breathing and Daoist breathing we talked about in the last section first, so you can be sure that you're breathing from your abdomen and getting the best amount of air and qi into your lungs and around your body.

Cleansing Breathing

Cleansing breathing is a very good habit to get into. Most people don't tend to empty their lungs completely when they breathe. This can be down to habit, or it can be because of stress. They're in such a rush to take another lungful of air that they don't allow the process to complete fully before starting again. Cleansing breaths can help you to get rid of stagnant air, and therefore stagnant qi, from your lungs, allowing fresh and clean oxygen (and qi) to enter.

Many people tend to hold tension in their shoulders, neck, and back too. If this is your situation, you may find that cleansing breaths will help to alleviate that problem. As you're breathing, focus on the tension ebbing away with every exhale.

To take cleansing breaths:

- Place your hands on your abdomen to make sure that you're breathing from the right place. As you become more experienced, you may not need to do this anymore, but it's a good exercise for a beginner
- Breathe in through your nose for a count of eight, feeling your abdomen expand
- As you inhale, notice the sensation of your lungs filling up with air until they feel full
- Exhale for a count of sixteen, noticing your abdomen deflate as you do so
- Feel your lungs emptying as you exhale until you feel the sensation of your lungs being completely empty
- Inhale again when you feel that empty sensation
- Repeat as many times as you need.

Original Breathing

Original breathing is very similar to Buddha breathing, and it is considered the main focus of QiGong breathing techniques. The name derives from the way in which a baby breathes when it first comes into the world and takes its first breaths. A baby hasn't learned bad habits when it comes to breathing, and they don't understand the concept of stress. They breathe in the most natural and easy way possible.

A baby's abdomen inflates like a balloon when they inhale and flattens completely as they exhale. That's exactly what original breathing looks like and how your body should appear when practicing this breathing.

The best starting point for original breathing is either standing up straight or sitting on a chair or a cushion. You need to be as comfortable as possible, just like a baby without a care in the world, but your spine should be extended so qi can flow freely. However, avoid tensing or sitting/laying in a position that doesn't feel natural to you. It's good practice to keep your spine straight, for sure, but forcing it will also affect the flow of qi. You need to find a happy medium.

To try original breathing:

- Place your hands over your navel and close your eyes if it feels more natural to you
- Before you do anything, become aware of your breathing
- When you're ready, tell yourself that you're going to breathe for longer and deeper. The intention is part of awareness
- As you inhale, fill your abdomen with oxygen and qi. Notice how it feels when your stomach expands
- As you exhale, notice as your abdomen deflates and how relaxing it feels.

You can carry on with original breathing for as long as you want. It's a very uplifting and relaxing thing to do, and if you're struggling with stress or anxiety, it's something that will certainly help. As you practice, you won't have to focus quite so much, and you'll notice that it becomes a natural process.

Tortoise Breathing

The next breathing technique we're going to talk about is called tortoise breathing. This is a good option for beginners, but you may find it helpful to lay down somewhere comfortable, flat on your back. Again, make sure that your body is in alignment, and your spine is completely straight. This shouldn't feel unnatural or painful, it should feel comfortable, and you shouldn't feel any tension in your back, neck, shoulders, or along your spine. The key to tortoise breathing is to make sure that you stay relaxed throughout.

The name comes from the way your body looks when your stomach is expanded, full of air, like a tortoise's shell.

To try tortoise breathing:

- Lay down somewhere comfortable, make sure that your spine is straight and you feel comfortable
- Breathe in slowly through your nose. You should feel your stomach expand as you do so
- When you feel that your lungs are full of air, wait for a second
- Exhale through your mouth slowly, pushing the air from your lungs out through your mouth. As you do this, your stomach will flatten
- Wait for another second and then repeat the process

Tortoise breathing is ideal for calming down during a stressful time, but it's a very effective way to absorb qi and focus your mind on the positive elements of life.

Kidney Breathing

We've already spoken about how different organs are related to yin and yang, and the free flow of qi can help to ease certain problems. Kidney breathing, as the name suggests, helps with kidney function as well as increasing lung capacity.

When you breathe in during kidney breathing, the lungs pull in qi, but the kidneys draw the qi down from the lungs so that it spreads further down into the lower reaches of the body. This energy is stored within the kidneys, growing and becoming stronger, but eventually, that energy becomes stagnant and needs to freshen up and move on. Kidney breathing helps to recharge the energy stored within the kidneys.

It's a good idea to start kidney breathing after you've done a few rounds of the original breath, but you can do it alone if you'd prefer. The best position for this breathing technique is standing up, but as before, make sure that you're relaxed with a straight spine.

To do kidney breathing:

- Stand with your feet parallel to one another, about a shoulder-width apart, and bend your knees very slightly to keep them soft and comfortable. Make sure that you don't move forward slightly as you do this; you need to keep that spine straight and upright!
- Move your hands, so they rest on your lower back, with the palms resting on your back, just above the level of your hips. Your fingers should point downward, toward the base of your spine
- Slowly tuck your tailbone under and your spine should lengthen and straighten a little more - it should still feel comfortable, however
- As you breathe in, move your lower back slightly so that it expands to let in the flow of energy toward your kidneys
- As you breathe out, relax and feel the energy flow a little more, with the breath leaving your body
- As you become more comfortable, tilt your hips slightly by contracting your abdominal muscles. Don't worry that your abdomen doesn't expand as much; it's not able to in this position, and instead, the oxygen will go back toward the kidneys instead, giving them a good massage, along with the nearby adrenal glands.

Kidney breathing is a good option for anyone who has lower back problems or for those who need extra support in the lumbar spine area. The gentle massage to the kidneys and adrenal glands will help to filtrate the blood and get rid of any toxins, while also regulating hormones in the area, thanks to the adrenal glands receiving plenty of nourishing qi.

Embryonic Breathing

Our final breathing technique is embryonic breathing, which is sometimes known as umbilical breathing or primordial breathing. However, they are the same technique.

This type of breathing has a back story. When we are in our mother's womb, we take in oxygen and nutrients through the umbilical cord. However, when we're born, that cord is cut, therefore severing that connection. At that point, we breathe in through our noses and mouths independently. According to Chinese medicine, a short while after a baby is born, the energy circuit divides into two meridians, known as Du and Ren. These were once one, and the connection is severed, creating two new meridians.

Embryonic breathing is part of the microcosmic orbit, an important technique in Taoist energy cultivation. This is when the Ren and Du meridians connect once more, creating a circuit and allowing energy to flow freely again. It takes us back to the same kind of state that was dominant during our time in the womb.

The more you practice embryonic breathing, the more those meridians will connect and boost your qi flow. This technique is best used with visualization alongside it. However, this particular visualization is very easy and something you can use to further your practice in meditation and visualization as a whole.

The best position for embryonic breathing is sitting in a chair, feeling comfortable with your spine straight and relaxed.

To try embryonic breathing:

- Turn your attention to breathing from your abdomen for a few minutes before you begin. You can place your hands on your abdomen if that helps you to focus

- When you're ready, on your next inhale, feel the stomach expand
- When you exhale, feel your stomach deflate but also contract your pelvic floor muscles (around the perineum) just a little. This doesn't have to be a full squeeze; just a very small contraction is enough
- On your next inhalation, imagine that your breath is a ball of light, pulling into your stomach and filling up the space
- As you exhale, imagine that ball of light squeezing smaller and contracting, remembering to contract your pelvic floor as you exhale
- Continue the cycle and imagine the ball of light becoming brighter as time goes on.

Embryonic breathing can be a little complicated at first because there is a lot going on. You need to remember to contract your abdominals, and pelvic floor on the exhale, while imagining the ball of light squeezing. That takes practice, so don't worry if, at first, you don't quite master this type of breathing. However, practice makes perfect, so don't give up!

The idea with embryonic breathing is that we're reconnecting with that cord that was cut at birth, therefore reconnecting the two meridians and allowing energy to flow freely and powerfully throughout the body.

Reverse Breathing

Reverse breathing is a little like Daoist breathing, but with a little more detail added. It is a very useful breathing technique for those who are struggling with anxiety and stress, but it is also known to help strengthen the core and abdominal muscles while giving the immune system a boost. This type of breathing strengthens the lungs and increases their capacity too.

The best position for reverse breathing is to sit down on the floor, so you can feel a strong and grounding presence below you. Place your legs on top of one another, so they're stacked in line.

To do reverse breathing:

- Place both hands onto your abdomen, with one above the other. Your thumbs should touch the navel in this position
- Breathe in and contract your abdominal muscles to pull inward, heading in toward your spine
- Breathe out and allow your abdominal muscles to release
- Repeat 5-7 times, until you feel relaxed and uplifted.

These breathing exercises are all beneficial in their own right, and they have different purposes. However, you can choose to practice any, at any time. If you're unsure where to start, first focus on the cycle of breathing, i.e., breathing in through your nose and out through your mouth, directing your breath to your abdomen. Those are the basics. From there, you can build on your experiences and expand your QiGong skills.

You can choose any of the exercises we've talked about in this chapter and practice. You might like to just focus on one for a while, or you might like to mix it up and try a few over the course of a week. Whatever works for you is the only answer to this. If a particular breathing exercise is calling out to you, give it a go and see where it takes you.

Points to Remember

In this chapter, we've talked at length about breathing. You might assume it's the most simple and effortless thing in the world, and in many ways, it is. But, breath is more than just oxygen. It's a vital rhythm that connects us to our bodies and the world around us. It's a way to create and pull in vital energy, and it's a way to affect how we feel and deal with difficult situations in life.

71

Breathing exercises are an integral part of QiGong. Practicing these exercises will give you a great grounding and will allow you to take your efforts further, therefore bringing more benefits to your life.

The main points to remember from this chapter are:

- Breathing techniques are a vital part of QiGong, along with movement, poses, and visualization/meditation
- We need to breathe to stay alive, but it is the one thing that is with you from birth until death
- How we breathe can alter our mindset and our emotions
- Most people breathe in a shallow manner naturally and don't get enough air and energy into their bodies
- Breath can be used as a grounding tool, helping us to cope with stress and anxiety
- Learning to breathe into the abdomen can help to expand lung capacity and cultivate more energy
- Breath can be used as an anchor and grounding tool whenever you need it, but it's particularly useful when practicing QiGong
- Buddha's breathing and Daoist's breathing are the basics of QiGong breathing techniques
- The 'correct' way to breathe in QiGong is to breathe in through the nose and out through the mouth, expanding the abdominal muscles and allowing them to retract on the exhale
- Visualization and breathing techniques used together are particularly powerful
- Emptying your lungs of stagnant air and energy is important, so make sure that you fully empty your lungs on every exhale
- There are different breathing techniques to try, including embryonic breathing and kidney breathing, and it's a case of trying different ones and finding what suits you best.

Chapter 6:
Introducing The QiGong Diet

Every day we eat meals to give us energy. You might assume that the energy you're creating is simply to fuel your body and allow you to go about your daily business. But, it's about more than that. You're not only fueling your body with nutrition to allow your body to function - food also allows you to take in extra qi, therefore enhancing your overall health and wellbeing in a more spiritual manner.

There is no specific diet for QiGong in a conventional way. That's to say, there is no list of foods you should avoid and enjoy, and there are no rules that you have to follow. If you picture the Keto Diet or the Atkins Diet, it's nothing like that. Instead, the QiGong diet is more about a set of general guidelines you should bear in mind when going about your daily life. This shouldn't feel forced, and you shouldn't put too much emphasis on it, but it should still be in your mind.

The truth is that once you get into QiGong, you'll want to eat in a healthier way generally. You'll want to keep the good results going, and you'll learn the difference between feeling great and feeling not so wonderful. You won't want to jeopardize that by eating a fat-laden takeaway that does nothing but fill your cells up with fat globules and zaps your energy on many levels. Instead, you'll want to continue feeling wonderful and see how far you can take it.

The good news is that it's not so difficult. The QiGong diet is simply eating healthily and bearing in mind a few other things. So, in this chapter, that's what we're going to focus on. By the end, you'll understand what a healthy, qi-gong lifestyle looks like, and you'll no doubt be keen to start yourself.

Eating in Line With QiGong

We know that there is no specific diet for QiGong, but there are general guidelines that help you to boost your energy cultivation efforts. Specific foods can boost your efforts or hinder them. When you're practicing QiGong, you'll want to maximize the amount of qi you're creating and allow it to run freely through your body. That way, you grab the benefits on a greater level.

Perhaps we shouldn't call them guidelines, and instead, we should say principles. You don't have to follow these particular ideas when you're practicing QiGong, but by doing so, you'll notice that you feel better and you're not semi-wasting your time.

We know that QiGong takes into account the body and the mind in one whole practice. It nourishes every aspect of your being - physically, emotionally, spiritually, and mentally. It does this through the flow of good quality, easy moving energy.

Nutrition, in general, is about how a food interacts with the body and the benefit, or otherwise, it brings. The principles of QiGong can be used in the same way when deciding what to or not to eat. It's also about how you cook food and how you eat it too. That's what we need to delve into further.

To break it down, when eating in a QiGong way, you need to look at the nutrition that will give your body what it needs, but you'll also look at the way energy (qi) affects your body and the different areas you want to target. Different foods stimulate your body in different ways, therefore reacting and using the nutrients effectively or not.

To understand how to follow the QiGong way of eating, you need to take into account the previously talked about philosophies of yin and yang, the seasons, the elements, and how they interact with specific organs. It may sound complicated, but it's actually much simpler than you might think - that's what you'll come to understand by the end of this chapter.

Elements And Seasons

To understand how food plays a role in the cultivation and flow of qi around the body, we need to examine the yin and yang philosophy once more, and we need to think about the elements.

If you remember from our earlier chapter, there are five elements that work together in QiGong. These are metal, earth, water, fire, and wood. These elements are connected to different colors, seasons, flavors, and different bodily organs. Foods fall into this too, ensuring that if you want to focus your energy on a specific part of your body, e.g., if you have kidney problems, you'll want to focus on that body part, you can do so by identifying the element and foods to eat.

- Earth is associated with the stomach and spleen, the color yellow and sweet flavors
- Metal is associated with the large intestine and the lungs, the color white, and spicy or acrid flavors
- Water is associated with the bladder and kidneys, the colors blue and black, and salty flavors
- Wood is associated with the gallbladder and liver, the color green, and sour flavors
- Fire is associated with the small intestine and heart, the color red, and bitter flavors

That explanation should give you some idea of how to start eating in a QiGong way from the start. For instance, if you want to target your liver, you'll focus on sour flavors and foods with a green color. That doesn't mean you should base your entire diet around this, as that's simply impossible and won't give you a full range of nutrients for the rest of your body, but you should incorporate these into your diet as much as you can.

If you want to target the flow of energy to your heart, you'll need to incorporate bitter flavors and the color red. This ensures that yin and yang are in balance and the philosophy that is so deeply connected to all traditional Chinese medicine methods is flowing as it should.

The reason why explaining QiGong overall as a concept is a little difficult is that it's so personalizable. There isn't a strict way to do it that must be followed at all times. It depends upon your desires and the outcome you want as to what you do and how you do it. There are, of course, principles and guidelines to follow, but no solid rules or a 'one rule for all' approach. The same goes with what to eat. Perhaps the only advice you can give that's across the board is to eat healthily and to avoid processed and high sugar foods. This is simply common sense and something that we should all be doing anyway.

What you can do, however, is target the areas of the body you want to focus on with your approach. That's the personalized side of it and something we can't explain to you and give you a direct plan. You need to work out your aims for yourself and then follow the principles and guidelines to come up with a way that works for you.

The reason we talk about the color of foods is that they tend to have different levels of nutrition according to the shade. For example, yellow foods tend to have specific nutrients within them, and red foods have different types of nutrients they specialize in. Those are likely to be the nutrients required for the healthy running of the organ that is attached to that element.

Flavors matter because our bodies react to flavors in different ways too. For instance, when you eat something sour, you salivate and eat differently, as opposed to when something is salty or sweet. This also affects how you ingest and digest them too, extending to the organs that you use when digesting food and for the absorption of nutrients.

While you can and should look at the specific organs you want to boost and choose colors and flavors attached to them, you should also make sure that you get a balance of the colors too. That way, you're getting a wide range of nutrients, and your entire body is functioning in an optimum manner.

Yin and yang come into this in terms of the temperature of the food. That doesn't mean how hot or cold it is when you've cooked it; different foods tend to raise your body temperature or cool it down, and that affects how it draws energy in or out of your body. This is also affected by how we cook food too.

Of course, foods that are coked are warming, and anything that we eat cold, e.g., raw food, will be cooling. This affects the seasons because you will make different decisions on your diet according to how hot or cold it is outside; when it's cold outside, you're more likely to want to eat stews and soups to warm you up. When it's hot outside, you'll want salads and fruit to try and cool you down.

If you live in a part of the world that is naturally hot, you'll find that the foods grown there are perfect for thriving in that specific environment. That's why one of the principles of QiGong eating is to go for seasonal, freshly grown produce. By doing that, you're remaining in harmony with the environment around you, and you're not consuming food that has been imported from countries thousands of miles away, therefore allowing foods to lose their freshness and nutrients en route.

It's a false idea that to follow QiGong, you need to eat in line with what is natural in China. Yes, QiGong is a traditional Chinese medicine method, but that doesn't mean you need to eat as though you're in China to make it work for you. That would simply be unrealistic because many of the foods that are naturally produced in China are very difficult to find in other countries and would obviously need to be imported. In that case, they wouldn't be as fresh or as nutritious, therefore not holding as much energy within

77

them. You're basically going against the whole idea of QiGong by assuming that.

Instead, you should focus on what is natural where you live and do your best to incorporate that into your diet. A little later we will talk in more detail about the types of foods you could go for, e.g., how to find them, how to prepare them, etc. For now, know that by eating seasonal produce, you're already starting in the best way possible.

Becoming A Mindful Eater

QiGong eating isn't just about choosing what to eat and making sure that it's fresh and full of nutrition. It's not just about choosing foods based on their flavor and color, in line with your health-related aims. It's also about how you actually get the food into your body.

When eating in line with QiGong principles, you have to remember that you also need to nourish the mind as well as the body. So, when you're eating your food, you need to know that you're not simply digesting food and taking in nutrition from whatever you're enjoying, you're also digesting your emotions too. To feel good on the inside, you need to be positive. That means you need to adjust the way you eat and show gratitude at all times.

Why should you show gratitude when eating?

Well, firstly, not everyone has the good fortune to have a meal to eat every day. Some people are going hungry, and you're not. That's the first thing to be extremely grateful for. Secondly, when you eat with gratitude in mind, you're focusing on positive emotions. When you think in a positive way, chewing your food and swallowing it down to be digested, you're also absorbing positive energy too. You need to harness nourishment from your emotions as well as your food.

Eating with gratitude can be done in two ways - expressing gratitude before you eat and throughout, and through mindful eating too.

Expressing Gratitude

The idea of expressing gratitude before you eat probably brings up the idea of saying 'grace' before you eat. You don't have to do this in a religious way to express gratitude. You can simply give thanks for what you're about to eat in a way that shows you're simply happy to have food on your plate. That helps to cultivate the positive emotions within you, which will help to free up blockages and allow qi to flow freely. It also sets the tone for the meal you're about to eat, therefore allowing you to digest and take in the nutrients required for good health and wellbeing.

You can say your 'thank you' aloud or in your mind - how you do it is up to you. It's also not about saying thank you to a higher power or any particular being; it's about simply taking a moment to be grateful for what you have.

As you're eating your meal, notice the flavors and think about how great it is to be tasting them and how wonderful it feels to try something so delicious.

Eating in a grateful way doesn't have to be difficult; in fact, it's not at all. It sounds like it should be something otherworldly or religious, but simply being grateful for having a meal in front of you doesn't have to be either of those things if you don't want it to be. By being grateful, you're doing a lot to enhance the positive energy around you, which will make its way into your mind and body as a result.

Mindful Eating

Mindfulness is such a positive habit to get into. Far too many of us are stuck in the past, or we're constantly jumping forward to the future. We don't take a moment to correct that and make sure that we stay firmly in the present.

Always thinking over the past creates a negative mind and causes you to live in regret. Jumping forward to the future also creates that negative thinking loop and causes you to feel constantly anxious. You can't go back and change the past, and even if you plan and work hard for the future, there are no guarantees that it will work out the way you want it to. For that reason, living in the present and making it as beautiful as possible is the single best way to live.

While there are many events to mindfulness, mindful eating is probably one of the easiest and most effective to try.

When you eat, do you rush your food down and then go about your day? That's something most of us do. We assume that we need to quickly eat our food and then get on with the never-ending 'to do' list we have on the go. By doing that, you're totally missing the point of eating. You're not nourishing your body in the right way, and you're certainly not nourishing your mind either.

You might also force yourself to eat simply because it's a specific time of day, even if you don't feel hungry. Look at it this way - you wouldn't attempt to sit down and have a heart-to-heart with your partner about an important issue just before you need to leave for work, and they're obviously half asleep, would you? You would choose your time wisely. That's what you need to do when eating.

Eating a meal should be a sacred experience. It should be something you do for pleasure, to enjoy the taste of the foods you're consuming, but it should also be a spiritual experience in terms of nourishing your mental and physical health too.

That is what mindful eating can help you with. It basically slows everything right down and causes you to focus your mind on every single aspect of eating. The Taoist suggestion is that you should take a bite of your food and chew for 50 times before swallowing. Of course, that does sound like quite a lot, and at first, it may be too much for you. However, you should aim for half of that and then build up as you become more experienced in mindful eating.

The idea behind this is that most people simply put the food into their mouth, usually too much at one go, and then chew quickly a few times and swallow before loading up their fork and repeating the process. There is no thought to enjoyment or the nourishment of the body and mind.

When you chew more, you're forced to focus on the actual process, and as such, you notice things that you probably didn't take any notice of before.

When eating your food, you also need to turn your attention to:

- Flavor
- How it feels in your mouth
- Texture
- How your mind feels when you're eating
- How your body feels when you're eating

Here is an example.

You take a piece of food on your fork and you place it in your mouth. As you bring the fork up to your mouth, notice the colors in the food and the smell. Then, place it onto your tongue and notice how your mouth naturally salivates according to the food you're eating. As before, different foods will create different reactions. Then, start to chew, remembering to chew at least 25 times for each mouthful.

As you're chewing, notice how the food feels, how it tastes, the textures and any smells you can still recognize from the food on your plate. This will give you a full sensory experience for every single mouthful.

When you've chewed enough times, swallow the food. Notice how the food feels as you swallow, notice your throat contracting, the food making its way down your throat and into your stomach. Be aware of any sensations you can feel and how your mouth feels now the food has gone.

When you're ready, repeat the process.

As you're eating, also be aware of how your stomach feels. Are you full? Are you still hungry? Do you need to drink some water?

Remember that the process of digestion doesn't start in your stomach; it starts the moment you put the food into your mouth. Salvation and chewing help to break down the food, making the job easier for the rest of your digestive system. Quality of chewing is important because swallowing half-chewed food makes it much harder for your stomach. That's why you may get that 'heavy' feeling in your stomach after eating quickly, or excess gas as a result of overloading the stomach too quickly.

Mindful eating, therefore, helps with the digestive process, but it also gives you the time to slow down and enjoy the food you're eating. You should also take the time to visualize the flow of energy as you're eating your food, as your body absorbs the qi from the fresh food you're consuming.

It's true that mindful eating won't feel particularly natural at first. It may seem like an effort, but you have to persevere and stick with it. Over time, you'll start to really enjoy the process, and the flow of energy will improve as a result.

Of course, most of us eat our meals with our friends or family members. You can still practice mindful eating if that's the case. However, at first, you might find it easier to try eating alone, just until you get the hang of it. After that, it should seem like a natural act that you do without thinking. You could also get your nearest and dearest to try it too!

Preparing Your Meals

We've talked about how you eat in terms of mindful eating and slowing things down, but we need to think about what you eat, how you prepare it, and touch upon the subject of beverages too.

There isn't a huge amount to bear in mind when eating in line with QiGong. It's really about understanding what is beneficial versus what isn't. When you've got that in your mind, the rest should be pretty simple.

Of course, we all know that processed foods and anything laden with sugar and fat isn't great for our health. The problem is that these types of foods tend to taste pretty good, and we crave them, e.g., cookies, chocolate, pizza, bread, etc. The key here is moderation.

Eating in the QiGong way doesn't mean you can never treat yourself. That would actually go against QiGong because it would block the flow of energy because you're miserable. But, this shouldn't make up the bulk of your eating, and it should certainly not become a regular thing. Instead, you should only treat yourself rarely and when you do so, make sure you enjoy whatever you choose to consume in a mindful way. Then, you'll truly enjoy the experience and take on board the positive energy associated with it. The key is not to make it a regular occurrence.

Instead, you need to focus on clean, healthy, and organic produce as far as possible.

The main guidelines are:

- Eat organic produce as much as you can

83

- Go for seasonal produce
- Eat raw foods as much as you can, as these retain much of their life force and nutrition
- Limit the amount of imported produce you consume and instead, consume produce from your local area
- Shop locally, rather than going for mass-produced produce from large supermarket chains
- Remember to aim toward the color and flavor related to the areas of the body you want to boost (the yin and yang principle we spoke about at the start of this chapter)

That's really the basis of how you should eat in terms of QiGong practices. Yet, we also need to think about cooking food. You can't eat everything raw. While you can eat many fruits and vegetables raw, you do need to cook some other foods for health and safety reasons. In that case, you should cook them in a way that retains as much of their flavor and nutritional value as you can.

There are specific nutrients that are particularly affected during cooking, and as a result, you should cook them in a way that limits the damage. The nutrients affected the most are:

- Vitamin A
- Vitamin C
- Vitamin B, including B1, B2, B3, B5, B6, B9, and B12 in particular
- Vitamin D
- Vitamin E
- Vitamin K
- Potassium
- Sodium
- Magnesium
- Calcium

As you can see, these are some of the most important vitamins and minerals we need in our diet. So, you should choose a cooking method that reduces the damage and retains as much flavor as possible. That also means not overcooking, which can take the nutritional value almost down to zero in some cases and will also affect the texture of the food and, of course, the taste.

A few good options include:

- **Steaming** - This is a healthy way to cook your food, and it's very gentle too, so it holds in a lot of the nutritional value.
- **Roasting or baking** - You can bake or roast your food with very minimal nutritional loss but do bear in mind that these cooking methods tend to affect B vitamins more than others. However, the losses aren't major, so roasting and baking are good options and one of the easiest ways to cook food.
- **Sautéing** - Sautéing your food is different from frying. When you fry food, you add oil and cook the food in that oil. When you saute, you simply use the heat from the pan, with nothing else added. Oil and fats can pull the nutrients out of food, and it's also not the healthiest way of cooking. Sautéing is healthier because there's nothing extra added, and it retains a lot of nutritional value, as long as you don't cook for too long.
- **Grilling** - This is another healthy option as you don't need to add oil or fat to cook your food. This is also a good way to keep nutritional value inside your food, as long as you don't cook for too long. Be sure to turn over halfway to keep things even.
- **Microwaving** - This might be surprising to you, as it's easy to assume that microwaving food effectively 'nukes' the nutritional value. That's not the case at all. As long as you don't use very high microwave temperatures, microwaving your food is one of the best ways to keep nutrition inside. You can also use a little water to basically create a steam effect, therefore retaining much of the nutritional value.

You also need to think about hydration.

Many of us forget to drink enough water throughout the day, and it's important to focus on good hydration as much as possible. However, when you're eating a meal, it's better to drink warm beverages, as opposed to cold ones. It may seem a little odd, but warmer drinks can stimulate the process of digestion and therefore ensures that you get more nutrition from your meals. That can also help to kickstart the flow of energy. On the other hand, cold drinks will dial down the effectiveness of your digestive process, meaning that you don't take in quite as much nutrition as you otherwise would.

Always Listen to Your Body

A very important part of QiGong, and general health overall, is to listen to your body.

Do you tend to eat until you're too full? This is something many of us do, and it's often as a result of eating too quickly and not taking the time to question whether you're full or not. Mindful eating is a way to counteract this problem, but you should always check in with yourself as you're eating your food to make sure that you're not overeating. That can leave you feeling sluggish and can also affect your digestive system in negative ways. .

Of course, you should also make sure that you've had enough when you're eating too! Underrating isn't healthy either. Make sure that you eat until you're satiated and then stop. Try not to make too much food when you're cooking, cutting down on waste and if you do have any food left, keep it in the fridge and reheat the following day.

Another bad habit in relation to food is skipping meals or even forgetting to eat. Are you guilty of this? The truth is that if you want to improve your health and wellbeing through QiGong you have to give it a helping hand. Make sure that you eat regularly, but again, don't force yourself to eat if you're not hungry. Basically, listen to your body.

Your body will tell you all you need to know. It will tell you when it's hungry, it will tell you when it's full, and it will let you know when it wants a specific type of food. Listen to your cravings and see if they're genuine nutritional needs or simply the result of a sweet tooth. Again, you can treat yourself in moderation; there's nothing to stop you from having a bar of chocolate in moderation occasionally, as long as you don't make it a habit.

The best question to ask yourself is, "am I about to eat this because I am actually hungry? Or, am I about to eat it for another reason?"

That's a good question to begin searching for your motivation more clearly.

It's also possible that you're not actually hungry at all; you're either bored or thirsty. Asking yourself that question will help you understand your reasons and help you sidestep anything damaging. For instance, some people are emotional eaters. It's a far better route forward to deal with the problem at hand than push emotions down by eating. That's not going to help with the flow of qi and will probably result in stagnant energy instead.

To cut down on the chances of simply being thirsty, which can sometimes disguise itself as hungry, try drinking a glass of water first and see how you feel after a while.

By listening to your body and addressing any problems, you can sidestep issues and make sure that you cultivate qi to flow freely. This will also ensure that you have a much healthier relationship with food as a whole.

Points to Remember From This Chapter

- There is no specific diet for QiGong. Instead, you need to focus on eating healthily and mindfully
- You can cultivate and absorb energy (qi) through your food
- The elements all have colors and flavors attached to them, giving you an idea of the types of foods and flavors you should go for if you want to address issues with the associated organs
- You should make sure that you cook and eat your food in a way that doesn't disrupt the nutritional values
- The temperature of food is also important for energy cultivation
- Eating foods that are natural to the part of the world you live in will ensure you get high nutritional value, without food needing to be imported and losing its quality
- Mindful eating will help you to slow down and enjoy eating your meals, noticing every single aspect of the process. This helps to increase energy flow
- Mindful eating will also help you to show gratitude for the food you have and the process of eating
- You should chew your food at least 25 times before swallowing
- You shouldn't force yourself to eat when you're not hungry - listen to your body and eat when your body asks you to
- Eat raw foods as much as possible, shop seasonally, and go for organic produce too
- Make sure that you cook your food in a way that doesn't damage nutritional value
- Remember to listen to your body and assess whether you're truly full or hungry.

Chapter 7:
Relaxation, Meditation, and Visualization

The final part of QiGong is meditation/visualization. This is the part that most people struggle with, purely because they have misconceptions around it or they struggle to shut out the noise in their heads.

The truth is that to meditate in any way, you really don't need to shut out the noise completely. Many people assume that you need to quieten your mind completely, with nothing coming in or out. That's a meditative state that only the most experienced practitioners can reach; it's completely unrealistic to expect most people to reach that point. What you can do, however, is reach a point that whenever a thought enters your mind, you can allow it to float in and out without feeling the need to do anything about it.

Meditation takes practice, and it's not something you'll feel comfortable with the first few times. The problem is that many people give up at that point because they assume they can't do it. Everyone can do it! You just need to persevere.

In this chapter, we're going to talk about the place of meditation, relaxation, and visualization in QiGong. You might not realize it, but when you're moving through the movements and using your breathing techniques, you're already halfway there. QiGong is a movement type of meditation; the exercises will help you to get into that meditative state in the first place, as you focus on how you move your body and the sensations you feel.

The Superpower of Meditation

Meditation is a word that encompasses many different ranges of the compass. It can mean sitting quietly and focusing on your breathing, it can mean using chants to focus your mind, or it can mean moving around and using visualization to help calm the mind, as in QiGong.

As we've already mentioned, many people think that meditation is just too hard. They expect results immediately (which is unrealistic), and when they don't come, they give up and assume they just can't do it. Anyone can do meditation, but it does take time and effort.

In QiGong, the meditation element is perhaps a little easier to achieve for beginners because you can focus on something to quieten your mind. In this case, that's the movements you're doing, breathing, and visualization. When you have all of those things to complete, it's easy to focus and not allow unnecessary thoughts to take up your time.

We know that there are different components that make up QiGong, but in terms of the meditation and visualization side of things, this is called passive QiGong. In many ways, it has a lot of similarities with regular meditation, but you can adapt it to your ability level, or you can simply find a way that suits you. Sitting quietly and focusing on your breathing is often more than enough to quieten the mind and concentrate.

Within passive QiGong, we have two specific branches to explore - ru jing, which focuses the mind, e.g., meditation, and cun si, which relates to visualization.

To show you how meditation doesn't have to be terrifying, let's take a look at a quick exercise to try.

- Sit down and close your eyes

- Think about your breath. Notice how when you breathe in your stomach expands and how when your exhale, it deflates
- Keep your attention on the inhale and exhale
- If any thoughts pop into your mind, don't pay them any attention; simply let them float in and out. That may be difficult at first, but it will get easier
- Sit in that breathing pattern for as long as you want to, although you may find it hard to focus for longer than a few minutes at first
- When you're ready to come out of your mediation, tell yourself that you're going to open your eyes and slowly do so.

That's how easy meditation can be. For sure, that's a basic exercise, but it's a good option for those who have never tried meditation before and want to start slowly and build up their confidence levels.

Another good option to raise general awareness and help you feel more 'at one' with your body is the body scan meditation. This is ideal for identifying any areas of tension or discomfort, and then you can focus your attention during your QiGong practice to help ease that discomfort and allow qi to flow more freely.

When attempting the body scan meditation, make sure that you have plenty of time to spare. You can't just squeeze in meditation. Sit in a chair, making yourself comfortable but also making sure that your spine is as comfortably straight as possible

- Close your eyes and turn your attention to your breath. It may be easier for you to place a hand on your abdomen, just as you did with the breathing exercises. You are aiming to breathe from your diaphragm, i.e., so your abdomen rises and falls

- Focus on your breathing and if you notice a thought trying to grab your attention, simply allow it to flow in and out of your mind - don't pay it any attention or delve into it at all

Focus on your breathing for at least 10 minutes, but try and go longer if you can. Don't push this too soon, however, as you may find that you become distracted more easily in five minutes before you need to leave for work. You need to have enough time to allow your meditation to take you where it goes, and you also need to have the freedom and space to relax. Time constraints and possible distractions will now allow you to do that. So, that means turning off your phone and making sure you lock the door!

Try this:

- Lay down on the floor and make yourself as comfortable as possible. You might like to try a blanket and make sure that your head is supported with a pillow. Close the curtains if you feel like the light might be a distraction
- Make sure that your legs are unbent, straight, and your spine is equally as straight. Your arms should be down by your sides
- Close your eyes and focus on your breathing for a few minutes, until you feel your mind start to become quiet. As with all meditations, if you notice any thoughts entering your mind, don't pay them any attention and instead let them drift in and out
- When you're ready, turn your attention to your toes. Become aware of your toes and scan them for any sensations of tension or discomfort. Scrunch your toes up and tense the muscles, holding it for a couple of seconds and then releasing it. Notice how relaxing the sensation is
- Then, turn your attention to your feet and repeat the process. Don't rush! Take your time
- After your feet, turn your attention to your ankles and repeat

- Then your calves, your shins, your knees, all the way up your body to the top of your head, not forgetting your arms and fingers
- Once you've scanned your entire body, you should feel extremely relaxed. Stay in that state for a few minutes, enjoying the sensation and feeling the flow of energy freely moving around your body
- When you're ready to move, tell yourself that you're going to open your eyes and move, signaling your attention. Do so slowly and allow yourself to sit for a few seconds before standing up.

It's good to get into the habit of meditating daily if you have the time. Ten minutes is all it takes if you choose the breathing example, and the more you do it, the more naturally it will feel to you. This will boost your energy flow and help you to develop a calmer demeanor.

In terms of the meditation you'll do when you're practicing QiGong, it's about visualization for the most part. These two elements work hand in hand to help focus your mind on the outcome you want to achieve - in this case, that's the cultivation and free flow of qi.

Relax ... It's Easier Than You Think!

The word 'relax' just sounds like it should happen naturally, doesn't it? The thing is, many people find it very hard to relax.

We all have busy lives, and sometimes when you're constantly switched on and trying to dash from responsibility to responsibility, it's hard to turn off your brain and chill out a little. You can also blame social media in some ways. We're always contactable, always connected, and that means you can never switch off and 'be' for a while.

But, if you want to live a healthier and happier life, you need to learn how to relax. This isn't just taking a little time out for the sake of it;

it's required for health and wellbeing. If you don't take the time to relax, you'll simply feel stressed and chronic stress over the long term is a dangerous road to go down.

The relaxation response is the opposite of the stress response.

When we're stressed, our bodies go into the 'fight or flight mode,' and that kickstarts hormonal reactions within the body, including cortisol (the stress hormone) and adrenaline. These are designed to help us fight the threat or run from it. But in reality, most things aren't a threat at all; our brains are very easily tricked in this regard. The opposite to this is relaxation, and that means you're able to stay calm and face issues without feeling the need to panic.

So, how can you relax? It's one of the stepping stones to being able to practice QiGong effectively, so learning how to relax is an important part of your journey. Of course, it will also better your life in many ways too and help to improve your mental and emotional health massively.

Spend Time in Nature

Natural surroundings are calming on so many levels. Make sure that you spend as much time as you can outdoors, breathing in the fresh air and getting plenty of natural light. Beaches, the countryside, mountains, even sitting in your garden, these are all ideal spots to recharge and feel much calmer as a result.

Focus on Your Breathing

How many times have we said this? Breathing is your anchor; it's something you can always rely upon. If you want to calm yourself down and relax, simply change the pattern of your breathing and slow down the rhythm.

Taking slow, long breaths is the ideal option here. This is the abdominal breathing method we have spoken about before. However, as you breathe in and out in this way, make sure that you focus entirely on the sensation of your belly rising and falling and disconnect entirely from any troubling thoughts or feelings.

Visualization

We're not going to dwell on this one too much because we're going to talk about visualization in much greater detail shortly. However, for now, understand that visualization is a very relaxing technique in itself. It takes you out of your current mindset and transports you somewhere else.

If you struggle with visualization at first, you could try guided visualization, either in a class or through a YouTube recording.

Body Scan Meditation

Remember the body scan meditation technique we talked about in our last section? That's a fantastic way to relax as well as making sure that you get rid of any kinks or blockages in your energy channels.

If you don't have the time to lie down and do the full meditation, you can simply focus on tensing up specific parts of your body and relaxing them. The release of tension will flood your body with relaxation and help you to reconnect with your body rather than troubling emotions that may be causing you to feel stressed or anxious.

Journaling

One of the main reasons that energy becomes blocked is down to negative emotions that have been held onto for too long. Journaling can help you to identify and let go of negative thoughts and emotions, and it can also be a very cathartic way to deal with issues.

You don't need to write an old-school diary if you don't want to; you can simply add in a few keywords or random sentences. The point is that you're writing down how you feel, and you can look back on it and identify triggers and issues that you need to deal with.

Essential Oil Massage

If you have someone willing to give you an essential oil massage, this can be an extremely relaxing way to unwind and also grab the benefits of essential oils.

Lavender is a good option for many different medical ailments, but it's also known to be perfect for de-stressing and helping with anxiety. Remember to dilute essential oils with a carrier oil, such as olive oil or sweet almond oil. Using essential oils on the skin undiluted can cause injury.

If you don't have anyone willing to give you a massage, you can use a few drops of diluted essential oils in your bath water and chill out that way, or you can topically apply diluted essential oils to your pulse points, e.g., your inner wrists, to help calm you down and help you feel relaxed.

Mindfulness

In our diet section, we talked about mindful eating. This is a form of mindfulness meditation, and it's an extremely positive way to live your life. Not only does mindfulness keep you in the here and now, but it's also relaxing because it stops you from stressing about the past and future.

Mindful eating is one way to do it, but a walking meditation is another very useful tool. All you need to do is head out somewhere quiet in a natural setting and focus on your breathing for a few minutes as you walk. When you're ready, look at your surroundings and pick one particular element. For instance, it could be a tree. Take in every single aspect of that tree, such as the powerful trunk and how it grounds itself into the earth, the way the leaves blow gently in the breeze, and the rustling sound they make as they move. Take in everything you can, and remember to avoid paying any attention to any other thoughts or feelings as you do so. Once you've finished with the tree or whatever you chose, pick another item and repeat the process.

Not only will you feel calmer and more relaxed, but you'll have been anchored firmly in the present for the entire process. The more you do it, the more 'in the moment' you'll be.

When learning how to relax, it's a good idea to try a few different techniques and see which one works for you. Don't just try it once and then decide it's not that effective, however; make sure that you give it a little time. Dedicate at least 20 minutes every day to relax and then build up as you see fit, and whenever you have the time. However, make relaxation a priority too; don't cancel your relaxation time because you're busy - that's completely going against the point!

The more you focus on the need to relax, the more it will become a natural part of your life, and that will ensure that your qi flow is free and easy.

Why Visualization Is Crucial

Finally, we need to talk about the big V - visualization.

Visualization is one of the key components in QiGong and works hand in hand with meditation. The two certainly overlap to some degree, and you'll find that focusing on picturing a scene in your mind's eye is actually a form of meditation.

Visualization isn't just using your imagination, but that certainly plays a part. In this case, you would use your imagination to set the scene, and you would then use your meditation skills to add extra detail, to really feel the picture you're creating, and to be 'in' it. Doing this helps to build a channel of energy that flows freely.

The more you use visualization, the more energy you will cultivate, and you'll develop a field of energy around you that protects you from negative energies. This is called your qi field, and the stronger it is, the more you'll draw from it and allow it to flow through your body effectively.

To visualize, you simply close your eyes and allow your imagination to flow, but you need to do it in a targeted way. Guide your imagination to picture what you want to see but also be open to your imagination simply coming up with new additions that perhaps you don't consciously think about.

The key is to always keep your visualization positive. Imagine places that bring you happiness and joy. This could be your favorite beach, a waterfall, a mountain scene that makes you feel at peace, anything that makes your heart soar.

Then, once you have the visualization in place and you're exploring it, use it to direct energy throughout your body. Feel it filling up your energy channels and soothing away your aches and pains. Feel it flowing freely to your organs and nourishing them with all the qi they need.

The great thing about visualization is that you can sit and do it at any time, anywhere, but you do need to make sure that you're not going to be interrupted because that will set you back, and you'll need to start all over again.

To get you started, let's look at a visualization exercise to try. You can use this opening visualization exercise before you begin any

QiGong movement or practice as it will start to get the energy flowing.

Choose a place that is beautiful and makes you feel happy. It's best if this is somewhere you've visited in the past as you'll be able to add as much detail as possible. Make sure that it is a natural place, including natural elements, such as water or earth. It's best if the weather is upbeat and bright, perhaps in spring or summertime, when energy is awakening and new life is being born.

Once you have your beautiful spot in your mind, you need to imagine yourself right in it. Don't just see it. Feel it. Notice the sounds, the smells, and the sensations all around you. Stick with this one place and don't move around and go somewhere else. You need to anchor yourself in this place of beauty, therefore connecting with the qi that the place holds.

- Stand with your legs a shoulder-width apart, and your knees very slightly bent for comfort
- Close your eyes and relax your whole body, making sure that your spine remains straight
- Place your hands over your heart chakra, in the center of your chest, also known as the Middle Dan Tian
- Start your visualization by picturing your place of beauty and see it through your own eyes
- Imagine that the sky is blue and the sun is shining down; you can feel the warmth from the sun over your body
- Take a deep breath and feel the calmness all around you, allow yourself to smile
- Examine the scene around you - what can you hear? What can you smell?
- Examine the energy vibrations around you - allow them to flood your body
- Feel the sunlight drenching your body and making your cells vibrate and glow

- Slowly, imagine that you're so drenched in the sun that you become the sunlight itself - you are one
- Once you're as far into the picture as possible, taking at least 5 minutes to explore, tell yourself that you're going to begin your QiGong movements and then get to it.

Remember your beautiful place and commit it to your memory. The idea is that you can use this visualization whenever you need to retreat somewhere calm and collected. You can also use this as your opening QiGong visualization, setting the positive scene for energy flow and cultivation.

You may find that visualization comes to you much easier than general relaxation or meditation. That's fine. You may find that it's more difficult for you, and you find other things easier. Again, that's fine too. Everyone is different, and we all have strengths and weaknesses. The good news is that you can work on it and improve where you are right now.

Visualization is such a key component of QiGong that you should certainly take your time in practicing and focusing as much as possible. You can be as creative as possible and add as much detail as you need to add. This is your picture and your place of beauty that you can retreat to whenever you want to or need to. Yet, don't make it too complicated as you'll probably struggle to remember the finer details. You'll know when to stop because the picture will simply feel complete to you - it won't be too cluttered or too sparse; it will simply radiate beauty and will make you feel at peace.

Without the ability to visualize carefully, you won't notice the same benefits from your QiGong practice. So, make sure that you dedicate time to this - it's one of the most enjoyable parts of the entire QiGong subject!

Points to Remember

And there we have it, our final chapter! It's been quite the journey so far, and it's only just beginning for you. In this chapter, we have wrapped up the final component of QiGong, the passive side - meditation, visualization, and relaxation.

Now, these sound like they should be easy, but many people struggle with all three. The problem is there are no step-by-step instructions on how to do any of them. It's just a personal deal. But, there are general guidance measures you can take to understand how to get started and what to do if you notice problems or distractions.

Without a doubt, meditation is the most troublesome aspect for most people, but with the few examples we gave you in this section, you should find that you have a starting point to focus on and work toward. You'll then see that, in reality, meditation isn't that hard - you just need a little time and effort.

The main points to take from this, our final chapter, are:

- Meditation, relaxation, and visualization are key parts of QiGong, and make up the passive element
- Many people worry about meditating because they assume that it involves chimes and chanting and the need to totally clear the mind. That's not the case; there are many different types of meditation that anyone can try
- When a thought enters your mind during meditation, don't pay it any attention - just let it float in and out of your mind
- You need to dedicate time and effort to meditation and don't simply give up because you didn't notice results the first or first few times
- Focusing on your breathing and the body scan meditation are great starting exercises and can also be very relaxing

- Ru jing is the meditation part of QiGong, and cun si is the visualization part; these both create passive QiGong
- Many people find it hard to switch off and relax, but it's important to make time for relaxation and place priority upon it
- The relaxation response is the opposite of the stress' fight or flight' response
- Journaling can be a good tool to help you identify negative thoughts and triggers, therefore blocking the flow of qi
- Meditation, spending time in nature, massage, essential oils, and visualization are all ways to relax
- Visualization is a key part of QiGong
- Visualization isn't just seeing a picture; it's about actually being' in' it and noticing how your senses interact with it
- Create your opening visualization exercise for every single time you want to relax or when you're about to start your QiGong routine - this should be a place of beauty that brings you joy, ideally in nature
- To visualize, you need to allow your imagination to run free!

Conclusion

We've reached the end of our book - congratulations! You now have all the knowledge you need to start on your own QiGong journey.

It's quite an accomplishment to reach this point. Most people don't bother to read a book to the end because they're not committed to the process. Yet, you're different. You're someone who wants to learn and grow. You want to know how to use QiGong to better your life and your health. By reading to this point, you've shown intention to the universe, and as a result, you have all the information you need to move forward and start taking major gains from your journey.

For sure, QiGong can seem complicated at first. When you opened this book, you probably had no idea what QiGong was, or you might only have had a slight inkling. Now you know all there is to know to get started. Of course, you can extend your practice as you learn and take on board extra advice from practitioners and other people who enjoy QiGong as part of their lives. This is a process that allows you to constantly grow and take on new ideas.

So, the first thing is to pat yourself on the back and congratulate yourself on reaching the end of the book and being someone who wants to grab the benefits of this ancient Chinese healing method.

The next step is to take on board everything we've talked about and to go out and start putting it into practice. Maybe you're still a little unclear on a few points, and again, that's no issue. You can go back and re-read any point again until it's clearer. This book will always be there for you to go back over if you need to do so. Allow it to be your guide and friend through your QiGong journey.

Did We Help You Understand QiGong Better?

It's true that some things may not be crystal clear for you just yet, but you should have the basics grasped and down pat. Of course, QiGong is made up of specific components that work together to create QiGong as a whole. They are movements, meditation, visualization, and breathing.

Every single element has its own challenges, but they all bring their own major benefits too. You can only benefit from those plus points if you really dedicate yourself to the cause. Ask yourself why you want to start on a QiGong journey and what it means to you. Keep that 'why' in your mind whenever you're looking for extra motivation. Because there will be times in life when you're tired or feeling down, and QiGong is the last thing you feel like doing. But, you must remember the way it makes you feel and how uplifted you are once you're done. That's something to hold onto and use it to motivate you to carry on.

You're not going to reach optimum health overnight. It's going to take time, but you're taking a step in the right direction by putting your time and effort into reading this book. That's not going to go to waste now - you have all the know-how you need to get started in a positive and firm way.

QiGong Has The Potential To Change Your Life!

It's true that what you've learned so far is about to change your life, and as you learn more, the possibilities are endless. You can also share your knowledge with those around you and allow them to embark upon their own QiGong journey too. If your family and friends are curious about what you're doing and what you're reading about, why not recommend the book to them? Then, you can help other people to become healthier and happier too. It's a win-win all around!

Remember, if you want to fully embrace the benefits of QiGong, you need to push aside any ideas you might have had before and focus on a positive mindset. Anything that cannot be proven by science is often dismissed by many people, but the truth is that QiGong has been helping people from all walks of life for years. It's true that this healing method has been around for far more years than we can count and probably even before that. Something that old doesn't stick around if it doesn't work!

By focusing on positive thoughts and a growth mindset, you'll find that you attract more free-flowing qi into your life, and it will nourish your body in all the ways it needs to. Ultimately, you won't regret the day you started QiGong, and you'll probably only wish that you had started it earlier.

But, better late than never, right?

Of course, your journey doesn't end here. In fact, it's only just beginning. We hope this book has given you the push you need to move forward and start using QiGong in your daily life. Start slowly, and don't allow steady progress to hold you back. It's easy to want to see fast gains, but the truth is that anything that comes easily simply isn't worth having at all! Instead, you need to focus on slow progress. That way, you know you're making progress that will stick and last. You'll remember everything, and you won't miss out on the smaller details that bring the big gains your way over time.

Remember, practice is what you need to focus on. New knowledge is about 90% practice!

Before You Go, Could You Do Us a Small Favor?

We've done all we can for you right now. We've given you all the information we have to hand, and now it's up to you to go forward and take it with you. Use it, share it, and expand upon it. Learn and never stop opening your heart to new advice. You can never know it all!

But, before we leave you to start your QiGong journey, we do have a small, teeny-tiny favor to ask you. Don't worry, it's nothing major, and it's not going to take much time out of your day.

Our aim is to spread the word about QiGong to as many people as we possibly can. We believe in the healing power and benefits of QiGong so much that we want as many people to take it on board and use it as possible. But, to do that, we need you to help us out.

How? With an honest review of our book.

Most people read reviews before they decide to buy something, be it a vacation, a new clothing site, or a book. You might have read reviews before you chose to pick up this book too. So, if you leave us a review that honestly tells people what you think, we can reach out to more people and help them to embrace QiGong too. You're going to be responsible for people gaining benefit!

Reviews are vital for authors because they help us expand and carry on writing content to help you in your lives.

So, if you feel that our QiGong book has helped you to grasp the subject and feel excited about the journey you're about to go on, we'd be extremely grateful if you could leave us a quick review. It needn't take more than a few minutes, and you can be as honest as you like! Feedback is always appreciated, and it helps us to understand what we can do better for you too.

What did you find useful? What do you think could be improved? What parts did you find the most enjoyable? What are you looking forward to learning about next? Let us learn more and carry on writing these books for you. And don't worry about nobody seeing your review - we read every single review and take your comments on board. Plenty of prospective buyers will also read it too. We're motivated by such useful comments and take great pleasure in reading every single one.

It's easy to leave us a quick review, depending upon how you're enjoying the book.

If you're using Audible, it's easy to leave a review. Just press the three dots that you'll see in the top right-hand corner of your device. Click 'rate and review' and then tell us what you think about the book. You'll be asked to finish off with a rating, anything up to five stars.

Are you reading on a Kindle or another e-reader? In that case, just head to the bottom of the book and swipe your finger up. The screen will change, and you'll be asked to leave your comments.

If, for whatever reason, these instructions don't take you to the review page, then head over to Amazon or whoever you bought the book from and leave us a review on the sales page.

We can't wait to hear what you think about the book, and your feedback will help us to carry on creating useful advice for people from all walks of life.

It's Time To Say Goodbye!

So, what now? Now we have to say goodbye.

You have everything you need to start on your new journey to enlightenment, awareness, health, and wellbeing. It's going to take time, but every single step you make will take you closer to your ultimate goal. Take every bump in the road with grace and see it as a learning opportunity. Understand that you're growing as a person and that QiGong will help you to reach your full potential.

Go back and check over anything that doesn't make clear sense to you, and reach out for extra advice from an experienced practitioner if you want to push your journey a little further. There are no limits to what QiGong can do for you; there are only limits on what you allow yourself to achieve.

With all the information you've learned so far and your motivation to get started, you have such an exciting future in front of you. Start slow, move at a pace that suits you, celebrate every small win, and don't allow any slight bumps to slow you down or hold you back. QiGong is a lifelong journey that allows you to reach higher levels of spirituality and wellness. People have been using this traditional Chinese medicine method for countless years and have taken major benefits as a result. You'll feel calmer, more within yourself, more grounded, less stressed, and healthier, and you'll have an abundance of energy as a result.

We wish you all the luck in the world and know that you're about to embark upon a journey of wonder and fulfillment.

Good luck!

INTERNAL TAI CHI

For Beginners And Intermediates

Powerful Tai Chi Chuan Lessons And Easy Exercises For
Adult & Seniors, Improve Your Memory, Mood, Sleep &
Flexibility And Find Grounding & Inner Peace

CHEN SONG

Table of Contents

Introduction

We live in stressful times.

At the time of writing, the world has just come out of a pandemic that caused millions to be put under strict lockdowns for weeks or even months at a time. The rising cost of living and high unemployment are also major causes of worry. Of course, even without post-pandemic issues, the world can still be, at times, a stressful place to be.

Few people really understand the impact of chronic stress. We're all aware of how unpleasant it feels, but stress can also manifest itself in all kinds of physical symptoms that can plague you over the long-term. It's sadly not a stretch of the imagination to say that over a long enough period of time experiencing large amounts of stress, the consequences can even become life-threatening.

This is why it's so critically important to find a way to manage and reduce our stress on all levels.

Of course, there are countless stress management techniques out there, some may seem rather basic while others are needlessly complicated. Talking about whatever is bothering you can be a great starting point, however if you want to truly battle stress and find lasting inner peace, how about trying a practice whose efficiency has been proven over thousands of years? In other words, how about getting started with Tai Chi ?

A Quick Introduction To Tai Chi

You may have seen something called Tai Chi on TV or in movies before. To the untrained eye, it can look a little weird, especially when you grew up with a western education. Once you try it though, you'll understand how powerful the calming effect it can have on the mind and body as a whole really is.

Tai chi is an ancient Chinese martial art that is thought to be more than 3000 years old. It was established during the Zhou Dynasty which ruled China around 1100-1221 BC. It is one of the oldest martial arts in the world, but don't let the phrase 'martial arts' fool you.

When we think of martial arts, we tend to think about karate or judo, basically a way to defend ourselves against aggression. While Tai Chi could potentially be used in that way, it's a far more internalized approach. Tai chi is first and foremost a philosophy and a way of life teaching calmness and focus.

It's no surprise then that Tai Chi has proven itself to be very effective for reducing stress in one's life and promoting a calm and centered existence.

Tai chi takes you through a series of gentle stretches and exercises, flowing from one posture into another without stopping. During a Tai Chi session, the body is constantly moving, albeit slowly and smoothly. The idea is to move in a mindful manner and to be aware of every motion. For this reason, you may hear Tai Chi referred to as 'meditation in motion'. The body and mind are connected, creating not only a great workout but also a calming and serene state for the mind to exist in.

Tai chi is:

- A fantastic way to battle everyday stress while getting a workout at the same time
- A way to boost strength and flexibility
- A method for grounding and calmness
- A great way to promote better sleep
- A way to clear the mind and focus on positives

The Intention To Change

Many people want to change their lives but don't do anything about the problem they're facing. For instance, someone may be feeling negative and down, but rather than look for ways to pick themselves up and make their lives a little more positive, they simply wallow.

In this situation, perhaps you're noticing that stress is starting to play a significant role in your life. You could sit and do nothing, allowing the current situation to continue in the same vein. Or, you could do something about it.

The fact you've picked up this book shows that you're someone who wants to change their current situation and improve it. You've shown a clear intention for change.

All of this means you're already taking leaps forward. Far too many people talk a good game but never do anything firm. You're showing you want to make a difference and by reading this book, you'll have the tools at your disposal to get up and do something about your stress levels.

There's no doubt that Tai Chi is a great way to reduce stress, but it's also an endeavor that will bring many other benefits too. Tai chi has long been lauded for its health-boosting effects. We know that when you feel less stressed, you're able to sleep better and your mood is lifted. When you're properly rested and you're getting regular exercise, your heart health is improved, your immune system is boosted, and the way you feel will push you to make even more positive changes in your life.

This Book Can Help You Change Your Life

I'm sure you have no interest in living a subdued or stressed life. You want to feel better both in yourself and with yourself. You'd love to possess a way to banish any form of stress from your daily routine.

If that is so, then you've chosen the right book to help you get onto the right track.

Throughout this book we're going to teach you everything you need to know about Tai Chi. It may seem like somewhat of a mystery right now, but we're going to break down that confusion block by block and help you to understand everything that makes this ancient art so special.

Once you understand what Tai Chi really is, and consequently what it isn't, you'll certainly be inclined to learn more and make it a part of your life. And you'll have both the knowledge and the confidence to implement a Tai Chi routine specific to your needs and desires.

We're going to teach you the basics, then we're going to move on to the poses that make Tai Chi a great workout too. You'll also learn about specific breathing exercises, as well as understand the key role of meditation. Many people are worried about this aspect of Tai Chi but the truth is that meditation can take many forms, and be as simple as just focusing on one thing with intent.

By the end of this book, you'll feel brimming with confidence and keen to start on your own Tai Chi journey.

Forget Your Preconceptions

Before we move onto our first chapter and learn the basics of Tai Chi, you need to do one thing. You need to erase any preconceptions about Tai Chi from your mind.

Tai chi won't work for you if you don't believe in it. For sure, you'll get a workout from the poses and the movement, but you won't benefit from the calming and stress-related benefits. A true belief that this is going to work for you is important if you want to gain full impact.

You've picked up this book because you want to avoid stress in your life as much as possible. You want to feel better and you want to boost your health 'by doing something positive in your spare time. Tai chi can tick all those boxes and add a few extra for good measure.

All you need to do is believe that this is the new endeavor for you and turn the page.

Chapter 1:
What Is Internal Tai Chi?

You've made a decision to keep pressing with your intention to try and master Tai Chi. Well done!

Now you need to focus your mind and start to learn more about the basics of this ancient and practiced art. As with anything new, having background knowledge can help you to not only understand better what you're doing, but it also helps you take on board the benefits more freely. When you understand something, you can see why it's helping you. That's a huge part of Tai Chi because so much of it is mental and emotional.

In this chapter, we're going to go over the basics of Tai Chi. We're going to tell you what Tai Chi is, and we're going to delve into more detail about chi itself. We'll also explain the link between Tai Chi and martial arts and a little about the history of this ancient practice.

If you want to get started on Tai Chi in a firm and most successful way, having a little background knowledge is key. That's what this chapter will give you.

Internal Tai Chi

You've no doubt seen Tai Chi in action before but you may not really understand what is behind this ancient practice.

Tai chi is an exercise that encompasses the mind and body. It started as a martial art in Ancient China. Nowadays, Tai Chi is practiced mainly for health reasons however you can use its principles to help strengthen the mind and body to continue your martial arts training.

Describing Tai Chi is complicated because for many people it's a feeling of peace and wellbeing. But of course, reaching that point requires you to actually do something and that practice is Tai Chi. To break it down in the easiest way, Tai Chi is a type of moving meditation. You will use gentle exercises that help to heal and strengthen the connection between the mind and body.

The overall aim of Tai Chi is to cultivate chi or qi, your life energy. Tai chi then helps chi to flow through your body and brings about the many benefits to your health and overall wellbeing.

With each smooth movement, seamlessly flowing from one to another, you will feel the building of chi within you and the inner relaxation is something that many people start to notice very quickly in their first few sessions.

Every movement in Tai Chi is meant to be slow and graceful. There are no stop points and no jerking movements, everything flows like water from one point to the next. The idea is to not only cultivate chi but to get it to flow as freely and as gently as the movements you're performing during your session.

A Tai Chi session will leave you feeling energized but relaxed. It's a strange combination of the two that most people cannot put into words. The session will help to balance yin and yang within you, two opposite life forces that need to be equally balanced in order for you to be healthy and positive in life.

Upon reading this, you may be concerned that Tai Chi is going to be complicated and many people worry about being able to turn off their minds and focus on the movements. You will quickly see that Tai Chi isn't that difficult and the more you practice it, the easier it will become to focus and follow the movements with grace and ease.

Many people start with zero knowledge and slowly build up to a journey that lasts a lifetime, enjoying Tai Chi regularly throughout their weeks. As you move through your Tai Chi journey, you'll quickly learn that there are many depths to this practice. You will learn a lot about yourself and your ability to be calm and mindful under pressure.

We know that Tai Chi is great for reducing stress but it is also a fantastic way to build your confidence and to help you handle the challenges that life throws your way.

The other plus point is that you don't need any specific tools to practice Tai Chi and you can do it anywhere. Heading out into nature is always a good idea because that helps you to connect with the earth's energy and boosts your own efforts, but if your living room is the only option, that's no problem at all. You can also exert yourself as much as you feel you can; Tai Chi is suitable for everyone because it can be adjusted to the individual's needs and preferences.

We're going to talk in more detail about the benefits of Tai Chi in our next chapter, so for now let's focus on the guiding principles that will help you understand Tai Chi a little better.

Guiding Principles

The guiding principles of Tai Chi form its very basics and the foundation on which you can build. These principles are all linked back to the basic laws of nature. This makes sense because nature and Tai Chi are extremely closely linked; that is one of the many reasons why you will see people practicing Tai Chi in the open air, often close to bodies of water or mountains.

Every movement is slow and graceful, as we've already explored, but this is key because it helps you to remain present in the moment. Your breathing will also be controlled and slow, keeping everything on the same level. Many people struggle with this at first, but it's important to persevere and try to keep your mind as clear as possible. If you do notice that you really can't stop thinking about the day you've just had, acknowledge the thoughts and allow them to float through your mind. The most important thing is that you don't become caught up in thinking about them too much or acting upon them.

The connection with nature is also ideal for slowing down and remembering what's important in life - another of the key principles of Tai Chi. We live fast and hectic lives, but when you're practicing Tai Chi, you'll notice that everything slows down, almost as if everything happening around you is in slow motion. When you're stressed and worried, this slow and gentle approach is something you crave.

To break down the main principles of Tai Chi, we can look at them in three main sections:

- Control of movements
- The structure of your body
- The body within

The Structure of Your Body

When practicing Tai Chi, it's important that you are mindful of your posture. You cannot practice Tai Chi when you're slumped or bent over. You need to be upright because that will allow the chi to flow down your spine and help to nourish all organs in your body.

One of the major benefits of Tai Chi is that it helps to improve posture, something most of us need. A lot of the time, we don't realize that we're slouching and this can cause aches and pains as we go about our daily business. In addition, slouching blocks the flow of energy throughout your body, causing disruption, unhappiness, anxiety, and stress.

A good posture is also important to help strengthen the muscles around the spine. This is another of the key health benefits. In terms of Tai Chi, it's not only about helping chi to flow, it's also about the fact that when you're standing upright, you feel tall and strong. You're positive and you're not doubting yourself, which is very important in practicing Tai Chi.

Tai chi also helps you to develop a better sense of balance, however when you first begin, you may notice that you are a little less stable on your feet as you move from one movement to another. This is normal and will improve over time, but by focusing on keeping a strong posture, you'll notice that your balance is much improved from the start.

The connection to nature here also relates to balance. When your body is strong and balanced, you're happier. The same can be said for nature all around us.

Control of Movements

We know that Tai Chi is a series of controlled movements that move freely and slowly from one to another. It's important that this is done slowly so you can reconnect your mind and body. When movements have a smoothness and slowness to them, they flow from one to another without any jerks or breaks. This maintains the free flow of chi throughout the body and helps it to gain momentum. Any jerk will break the flow.

When using the flowing movements, imagine that you're pushing against a very gentle type of resistance, such as water. This helps you to generate more chi as you move and the image of water helps you to reconnect with nature.

The Body Within

It's not all about the outer body, it's also about what goes on inside of your body too. When standing up straight, you may be tempted to lock your knees or overstretch when moving. This isn't something you should do. Make sure that you relax your joints and don't make movements that cause your ligaments and joints to stretch or jerk. The point is that you're soft and relaxed at all times.

However, one of the main principles of Tai Chi is that your movements are controlled. That means your joints should also be controlled; floppy joints do not give you control over your movements and will cause you to make jerky transitions from one movement to another. The idea is to stretch your joints but don't lock. Loose joints can be strengthened with Tai Chi practice, so if you struggle at the start, you'll notice that this improves as you persevere.

Tai chi is certainly about the mind and to develop the right mindset for Tai Chi, you need to achieve 'Jing.' This means that you're in the moment, mindful, and you're not distracted by what went on during your day or your general cares and worries. You'll find that once you focus on the movements, this is much easier to achieve.

These three principles of Tai Chi are integral to ensure that your practice is beneficial. They may seem easy but you should not underestimate their importance in improving your practice.

What Exactly Is Chi?

We've mentioned chi a few times, so let's concentrate on what that actually is during this section.

Chi or qi are one and the same thing - energy. When your chi is out of balance, it's not flowing freely, or you don't have enough of it, you don't feel well within yourself. You may also notice that you develop

127

physical ailments too. Many people struggle with lack of focus or irritability when they're experiencing problems with chi.

Chi flows through your body at all times, but the flow needs to be smooth for you to be healthy. Chi helps to deliver energy, nutrients, vitamins, and blood to all parts of your body, ensuring that you're fit and healthy and every organ is getting what it needs to function correctly.

The concept of chi goes back to traditional Chinese medicine, where chi is considered to be a major life force. Abundant, free-flowing chi is considered to be a mark of health and vitality. Chi flows by using meridians as a path. You might have heard about chakras and these are also connected with chi; when there is a blockage in one of your chakras, chi is unable to move through and can therefore manifest health problems in that particular area.

There are many things that can affect how much chi you have and how well it flows. We know that a poor posture can affect the flow of chi but there are several other factors too, including not getting enough sleep and clean water, a lack of fresh air, and a poor diet. If your basic human needs are not met or not abundant, your chi will be affected.

It's also no surprise that one of the effects of a lack of chi or a blockage is feeling stressed and overwhelmed. For that reason, Tai Chi can help to get your chi flowing freely and therefore alleviate the problem.

The Martial Arts Link

We've mentioned that Tai Chi started off as a martial art in Ancient China and that can lead to a lot of confusion. We know that Tai Chi is suitable for all, but martial arts most certainly aren't. So, what is the connection?

When Tai Chi was first developed, it was a martial art but not in terms of fighting. It was a mindset, a practice that helped fighters to practice and prepare for defense, helping them to move in an effective and energy efficient way.

Some people choose to do Tai Chi as a martial art, however most focus on the health benefits. If you do want to practice it as part of martial arts training, there are different stages you will need to go through. These are:

- Muscle strengthening, balance, and flexibility
- Relaxation to build up strength within
- Learning how to place your hands and feet to apply the correct amount of force
- Fitness training
- Improving focus and mental clarity
- Visualization to help with strategy
- How to absorb force and redirect it

Tai chi as a martial art is not the type of martial art you may have in your mind. It isn't like karate or judo, it's a practice that prepares those who want to fight. However, the overwhelming number of people who use Tai Chi do it for relaxation and health benefits only.

The Philosophy And History Of Tai Chi

It's interesting to learn about the history of a new endeavor you're about to incorporate into your life. When you understand something and its roots, you can apply it to your life far easier.

Tai chi is very closely linked to another practice, called QiGong. These are both based on traditional Chinese medicine and they date back thousands of years. The actual founding of Tai Chi is very unclear and you'll find many different takes on the subject. However, the general school of thought is that Tai Chi originated during the Zhou Dynasty, around 3000 years ago. At this time, the balancing of yin and yang was the main focus of Tai Chi, therefore boosting chi flow.

There are many other schools of thought, some of which are shrouded in legend. For instance, some believe that Tai Chi was developed by Zhang Shanfeng, a Taoist during the 15th century. Shanfeng was believed to be extremely strong and have almost superhuman skills. These were put down to Tai Chi and the use of Tai Chi as a martial art developed from there, as fighters wanted to experience the same superhuman strength as Shanfeng.

Whatever the actual starting point of Tai Chi, it certainly has strong links to taoism and Ancient China. It's older than any of us really know, but at least 3000 years.

The translation of Tai Chi is believed to be 'supreme ultimate', which can be taken in two different ways. You can see this from the martial arts point of view or you can look at it from a natural point of view. For those who practice Tai Chi for the relaxation and health benefits, 'supreme ultimate' is thought to be due to the balancing of opposites (yin and yang) and restoring harmony through a connection with nature.

Tai chi has been documented throughout history and it has always been a popular practice amongst those who want to focus on stress relief. Many celebrities have spoken about their own Tai Chi practice, which has pushed others to discover it for themselves.

What Are The Key Differences Between Qigong And Tai Chi?

QiGong is a very similar ancient Chinese practice that many people confuse with Tai Chi. There are key differences and it's important to know what those are, so you can ensure that you're following the right principles for Tai Chi and not becoming confused with the teachings and principles of QiGong.

Both are extremely beneficial to health and wellbeing and have very similar benefits, but Tai Chi is more about movement, whereas QiGong is more about poses.

QiGong is pronounced as 'chi gong' and it's also concerned with the free flow of energy (chi) throughout the body. The same principles of balancing yin and yang and chi flow are connected with QiGong, it's simply the application that is a little different.

Qi means 'chi' and gong connects to cultivating or working. That means QiGong cultivates energy and puts it to work. When performing QiGong, you need to use breathing exercises, visualization and meditation, a little like Tai Chi. This helps to solidify the intention and builds mindfulness. These concepts all help chi to flow more freely throughout the body.

The main difference between QiGong and Tai Chi is the movements performed. Tai chi is an ever-moving practice. Movements flow seamlessly from one to another without pause. The pace is slow and controlled at all times. However, QiGong is characterized by poses, i.e. stationary movements. These poses are repeated a set number of times in order to cultivate and move energy around the body.

The idea is that you can then send energy when your body needs it, i.e. if you are experiencing back pain, you can send chi to your lower back and therefore heal the discomfort.

Both QiGong and Tai Chi are excellent practices and both have a myriad of advantages. However, it's important to know the differences between the two if you're going to focus your efforts on Tai Chi only.

Points to Remember

- Tai chi is an exercise that bonds the mind and body

131

- Tai chi is thought to be at least 3000 years old, originating in Ancient China
- It was originally started as a martial arts practice but is mostly used these days for health
- Tai chi is a series of constantly flowing movements that move seamlessly from one to another
- Tai chi helps to cultivate chi (life energy) which then flows throughout the body freely
- Tai chi slows down the mind and helps to keep everything in perspective, reducing stress and anxiety
- During Tai Chi, yin and yang (opposites) are balanced for overall well being and vitality
- Posture is very important in Tai Chi; a slouched position can affect how freely chi flows
- It's important to look after yourself as this can affect the amount of chi you have flowing in your body
- During Tai Chi, you need to develop 'Jing'. This is a calm mindset and being firmly in the moment
- QiGong and Tai Chi are similar but they have different methods. QiGong involves static poses, but Tai Chi is about free-flowing movements.

Chapter 2:
How Can You Improve Your Life With Internal Tai Chi?

Now you know what Tai Chi is and where it came from, you're probably keen to learn more. The most common question about Tai Chi is "what can it do for me?" Of course, that's the main concern because nobody is going to dedicate time and effort to learning an ancient art if it has no major benefit to their lives.

The good news is that Tai Chi has many benefits for both mind, body, and soul. While it may take time for these benefits to become apparent, practice will certainly make perfect. The first few times you try Tai Chi, you may be a little preoccupied with focusing on getting the movements right and trying to keep your balance. This is normal.

When you first start, you will need to give it time. Tai chi has been practiced for thousands of years, which should give you a lot of confidence in its ability to make a change in your life. This is no flash in the pan idea, it's something which has lasted the test of time.

By persevering and giving it time, you'll notice that you feel calmer, grounded, more relaxed, and less stressed after a short amount of time has passed.

In this section we're going to explore the benefits of Tai Chi and how it can change your life. We're also going to reassure you that anyone can use Tai Chi to improve their overall health and wellbeing. Of course, a practice as old as Tai Chi is likely to have different forms and we'll outline those, to finish off your overview.

What Are The Major Benefits Of Tai Chi?

Tai chi has long been lauded as an effective and gentle way to reduce stress levels. Reconnecting with nature helps to ground you and by focusing on bringing harmony to your mind and body, you can understand why stress finds it hard to exist in such a situation.

However, it's not only stress reduction you can benefit from when you incorporate Tai Chi into your life.

In order to benefit from the major health plus points of Tai Chi, you need to focus on making it a regular part of your life. That means you need to dedicate time and effort a few times per week and really focus your mind on the positive elements of it working for you. We mentioned in our introduction chapter that you need to believe Tai Chi is going to benefit your life in order for it to do so. That's a very important point to remember.

If you want to accept the benefits into your life, you need to dedicate yourself to Tai Chi over the long-term. When you do that, the following benefits may come your way:

- Reduces stress and anxiety
- Increased fitness and aerobic ability
- An increase in energy levels
- A good way to reduce mild depression
- Improved mood in general
- Improved stamina levels
- May improve mild joint pain through strengthening
- Strengthened muscles and improved muscle tone
- Better flexibility and balance
- Provides a boost to the immune system
- May reduce blood pressure
- Deep relaxation and therefore better sleep quality

- Improved balance could help to reduce the risk of falls in older adults
- An overall improved sense of health and vitality

As mentioned above, benefits may not happen overnight but you will be able to sense a change in your overall demeanor because, at its very root, Tai Chi is exercise. Exercise makes us feel good and helps to release feel-good endorphins. When it comes to relieving stress, that's not going to go away overnight but with perseverance you will notice that your stress levels slowly start to reduce.

Practicing Tai Chi over the long-term maintains these benefits and ensures that you continue to take advantage of everything that Tai Chi can give you.

Is Tai Chi For Everyone?

Tai chi is a type of exercise and before you take on a new endeavor such as this, you should speak to your doctor if you have any particular health concerns. This is simply to get the green light to continue. We cannot give an exhaustive list of all the health concerns that may prohibit Tai Chi or cause you to alter the movements to suit your situation. However, for the most part, Tai Chi is generally safe for most people. Speaking to your doctor will give you the peace of mind you need.

Tai chi is very low impact and it doesn't stress the bones, joints, or muscles greatly. That means if you haven't done any exercise in a while, this is a good place to start. It's also a good option for older adults because it can improve balance and therefore help to reduce the chances of falls in later life. Many older adults also find that Tai Chi gives them a new lease of life in so many ways, thanks to the uplifting experience it brings.

Tai chi doesn't require any props or equipment and it can be done anywhere. That makes it a good option for people who can't really afford to pay for expensive gym memberships. However, if you prefer, you may join a Tai Chi group and learn with the help of a tutor and other participants in the class. If you prefer to do Tai Chi alone, that's perfectly acceptable too.

The truth is that Tai Chi is very adaptable and flexible. You can easily fit it into your routine and you can alter certain details to suit your needs. For example, Tai Chi can be done either indoors or outdoors. If the weather is a little cold or rainy, that means you can take your practice indoors and you're not missing out.

However, there are some contraindications to Tai Chi that we should mention. If you have any of the following conditions you should speak to your doctor before starting Tai Chi. In some situations, it may be that you can still go ahead with the exercises, you may simply need to modify some of the movements to suit your needs.

- Moderate to severe joint problems
- Persistent back pain
- A history of fractures or osteoporosis
- A hernia or a history of hernia
- You're pregnant

If that is the case for you, attending a class is a good idea in the first instance - after consulting with your doctor. This will help you to know which movements need to be modified and how, and you can then take that knowledge and continue your practice alone, if you prefer.

The Different Types Of Tai Chi

Tai chi is thousands of years old and that means it's likely to have changed and adapted over time. While the general principles and concept is exactly the same as when it was founded, Tai Chi does have a few different types to explore.

The main five types include:

- Chen
- Hao
- Wu
- Yang
- Sun

The names of the different types of Tai Chi come from ancient and influential families throughout Chinese history that developed the different styles. As with many things throughout history, Tai Chi is open to interpretation, while maintaining the basics. These five families changed certain parts of Tai Chi to allow it to fit in with their own interpretations.

Whichever option you choose, you're still doing Tai Chi. There aren't any that are better than others, however Chen is the original type. Despite that, Yang is the type that is most commonly seen in the modern day. Classes often teach either Chen or Yang, so if you do want to go to a class, you'll need to check beforehand which style they teach.

The only major differences between the different types comes down to the force of the movements, e.g. whether soft or explosive, and the positioning you use.

Let's look at each type in turn to outline the major differences.

Chen Tai Chi Style

Chen is the oldest type of Tai Chi and therefore considered the original. Many classes focus on the Chen style, however you should check if you do want to focus on another type, before choosing a class.

Chen is a mixture of slow and very gentle types of movements with occasional explosive and very fast movements. This is the oldest type of Tai Chi and the one that is as close to its origins 3000 years ago as possible.

Hao Tai Chi Style

Hao Tai Chi isn't as commonly practiced as Chen and Yang and you won't usually see it in classes. There is no solid reason behind that, it's simply that it isn't as popular as the other two. However, if you prefer to try Hao Tai Chi, that's entirely fine and you're still going to gain the benefits over time.

Hao Tai Chi is less about the power and size of the movements you're making and it's more about the force you use internally. For instance you will muster up the strength to make a movement and extend its intensity and power by manifesting the power within.

As you can see, this is likely to be quite a difficult style for a beginner.

Wu Tai Chi Style

Wu Tai Chi is another less common type of Tai Chi although you will find some classes that focus on this style as it's quite a useful option for older adults and those who have only just started exercising after a long amount of time.

Wu Tai Chi is very gentle and soft. Rather than focusing on explosive movements, instead it uses a different type of posture - leaning forwards very slightly and redirecting force, e.g. working against an imagined resistance. This type also uses a lot of visualization which can be difficult at first for beginners to master.

Yang Tai Chi Style

Yang is the most popular type of Tai Chi practiced in the modern day and especially in classes. Its name is from the family that created it, but it could also be a nod toward the balancing of opposites - yin and yang.

Yang Tai Chi generally contains movements that are gentle and have a large frame, e.g. they take up a considerable amount of space. Compared to Chen Tai Chi, there are less explosive movements and Yang Tai Chi is much slower and more relaxed.

Sun Tai Chi Style

The fifth type of Tai Chi is the latest interpretation of Tai Chi and it's quite a lively version. Movements involve more energy and are a little faster than Chen or Yang. Positioning is also a little different, with an extended, tall posture involved.

These five types of Tai Chi are all valid and useful in their own right. Because Tai Chi is a personal consideration, you may want to explore these types in more detail before deciding which is the best fit for you. Again, speaking to a Tai Chi instructor may be a good choice if you're not too sure. If you're not too concerned with type, Yang is likely to be the option that you find the easiest, or you could opt for Chen, the most authentic of all Tai Chi styles.

Whichever option you go for, you're going to find it a very useful addition to your life and all benefits still apply. The types simply differ in how you go about the practice, not in the benefits you receive.

What If You Never Clicked With Meditation?

At the start of the book, we referred to Tai Chi as a 'moving meditation.' That's the simplest and most accurate way to describe the practice. However, the word 'meditation' is somewhat misleading.

Tai chi does not require you to go into a trance or to completely switch off your mind and chant. Regular meditation, e.g. sitting on the floor and focusing your mind on one solid thing, can be very difficult for beginners. However, it's not impossible to teach yourself. One of the most common myths about meditation is that you have to completely quieten your mind to the point of being blank. That's not the case.

Only people with many, many years of experience in meditation can hope to reach such a point. Most people notice that thoughts venture into their mind during meditation and that's completely normal. We live in very busy times and your mind is always jumping back and forth, planning what you need to do and trying to remember things. While meditation aims to calm your mind and try to keep you in the present moment, it's very likely that your mind is going to have other ideas at the start, and perhaps even when you become a little more experienced.

The key is not to panic or assume that you've failed because your mind decided to intervene. You cannot fail at meditation. The worst thing you can do is assume it's not working and just stop trying.

In Tai Chi, you're not meditating in the usual way, but you are focusing your mind and moving as you're doing so. That basically means the same thing as regular meditation in some ways, just different in how it's practiced.

Focusing your mind isn't easy so do expect that you're going to have to keep reminding yourself to focus. Again, it's normal for that to happen.

The best thing is to pay no heed to any thoughts that enter your mind. Remind yourself that anything you need to do, you can figure out later. Right now, it's your time to relax. Acknowledge that you're having a thought, but don't analyze it or dwell on it. Certainly don't allow it to grow to the point where you're planning what to do about it. Let it flow in and out. With practice, this will become easier.

For many people who try Tai Chi for the first time, it's not getting the hang of the movements or balance that's the trickiest part, it's being able to stop thinking about everything around them enough to focus on what they're doing.

Breathing exercises are an integral part of Tai Chi and that's because they help to quieten the mind and relax the body. If you do notice your mind wandering, turn your attention to your breath and focus on that. Your breath will always be with you and it's a grounding tool you can use to refocus and bring yourself back to the present.

You don't have to have tried meditation before to start using Tai Chi. You will probably find that your mind is so focused on the movements you're trying to learn, that you aren't distracted too much. But, your breath will be the guide to help you, should you need it.

Introducing Your Tai Chi Practice Into Your Daily Life

Benefiting from Tai Chi requires intuition on your part. You need to allow it to become a part of your life and dedicate time and effort to it. You're not going to notice benefits if you try it only once every two weeks.

The greatest benefits come from regular Tai Chi over the long-term. This can be twice per week or more than that, but it has to be a regular part of your life in order for it to create a major change. This will also allow you to build your confidence and help you to explore other types of Tai Chi or more advanced movements.

You may find it easier to practice Tai Chi in the same spot. If you normally go into your garden for your Tai Chi practice, that will create a routine that gets you in the right mindset every time you head out into that space. That doesn't mean you can't mix and match if you want to, but a routine may be a good option if you are someone who struggles with focus.

If you have a busy schedule, e.g. you work shifts or you're simply busy with family and work, make Tai Chi a priority as much as you can. Even half an hour's practice is better than none. However, if possible, set aside an amount of time on specific days that you can look forward to as your time to switch off and relax. That will help you to see Tai Chi as a beneficial and enjoyable part of your routine.

When you're not in a situation where you can perform the moments, e.g. maybe you're at work or you're traveling, you can still use meditation and visualization to help you stay in the same zone and to cultivate chi to move throughout your body. Spend some time focusing on your breathing and visualize positive events occurring in your life.

A little later in the book we're going to talk about breathing exercises and these are things you can use at any time, not only when you're practicing Tai Chi movements.

If you want Tai Chi to become an integral and important part of your life, you need to make time for it.

Points to Remember

- Tai chi takes time and practice. Don't expect to be able to get it right straightaway
- Intention is essential - if you believe it will work, then it will
- To maintain the benefits, you need to make Tai Chi a part of your life over the long-term
- Tai chi is safe for most people, but you should speak to your doctor if you have any special health concerns
- Tai chi offers many benefits for the mind and body, including stress reduction, improved flexibility and energy, relaxation and immune system boosts
- Pregnant woman should also seek advice before trying Tai Chi
- There are five main types of Tai Chi, named after the founding families - Chen, Yang, Wu, Hao, and Sun
- Tai chi can be practiced alone or in group settings with a tutor
- Chen style is the most original, but Yang is the most commonly practiced type of Tai Chi
- Meditation can be difficult for beginners but it simply takes perseverance
- If you find it hard to focus and meditate during Tai Chi, or even outside of Tai Chi, simply turn your attention to your breath. This is a grounding tool that will bring your mind back to the present
- You do not need to completely quieten or block your mind to meditate, you simply need to avoid analyzing or paying heed to intrusive thoughts
- Make Tai Chi a priority in your life and set aside time to practice. If you're busy, practice as much as you can within your schedule.

Chapter 3:
Getting Started

Your first forages into the world of Tai Chi are important. These set the tone for the entire journey you're about to embark upon, but you should always remember that practice makes perfect.

You're highly unlikely to get your Tai Chi moves right the first, second, or third time. You need to stick with it and keep working on perfecting your movements and using your breathing exercises to stay firmly in the moment.

In this chapter, we're going to talk at length about how you can prepare yourself to get started with Tai Chi. The basics are extremely important because they lay the foundation on which you can build. You cannot build a strong practice from a shaky set of foundations. So, make sure you take the time to build confidence in your practice and know that the more you do, the better you will become.

We will then go on to talk about warm up and cool down exercises, the mental side of Tai Chi, and finally we will discuss large and small frame styles of Tai Chi. These are all important aspects of getting started, so make sure you take the time to build that strong foundation from the get-go.

Your First Steps With Tai Chi

We know that Tai Chi is a very widely accessible practice and most people can take part. You don't need to join a class, but if you prefer you can do so. However, most people choose to start in the comfort of their own home, or in a space nearby that they feel comfortable in.

In this first section, let's explore the very basics you need to start taking your first steps into the world of Tai Chi.

Find a Suitable Time And Place

Tai chi requires time and effort. That means you need to identify the best time for you to start practicing. Don't overdo it at the start - you don't need to practice every single day, but you should make sure to try at least a couple of times per week. Even when you're not physically moving, you can use breathing exercise to keep yourself in the right mindset and to remain calm and stress-free.

Don't decide to try Tai Chi if you need to go out half an hour later. You need to be able to clear your mind of distractions as much as possible, and the fact that you're keeping one eye on the clock isn't going to give you that chance. Instead, choose a time when you have no responsibilities for at least two hours. That should give you adequate time to focus and perhaps even become a little lost in your new endeavor.

The next thing is to choose the right place to start your Tai Chi. You will obviously need to be somewhere quiet and distraction-free. Don't attempt to do your Tai Chi in the living room while your family members are milling around the house. You'll only be distracted and that will cause you to stay half in and half out of the right mindset.

It's always best to try and be surrounded by nature if you can. If you have a back garden, that is the ideal spot if you don't want to venture too far away. If you have a beach nearby that's generally quiet, that is another great idea. Even a lakeside is a good choice. The point is that you need to be somewhere that you feel comfortable and a place that's not going to find you surrounded by many distractions.

You can do Tai Chi alone or with friends or family members. The choice is yours. However, most people prefer to try Tai Chi alone at first, as it allows them to focus and not to feel self-conscious in any way. Then, if you want to include other people in your practice and show them how beneficial Tai Chi is, you can do so.

Select Appropriate Footwear

Footwear is very important for a beginner in Tai Chi. You will see many people practicing Tai Chi barefoot, but for someone who is only just starting out, good footwear is the best idea. You may find that you slip or stumble otherwise, simply because you're getting used to the movements. It may also be that your balance and flexibility isn't the best and in that case, practicing barefoot will cause you to struggle. Your movements will not be as smooth either.

To counteract this problem, choose shoes that are comfortable and that have a rubber tread. You don't need anything too tight, so if you're wearing sneakers, be sure to lace them up just enough to be comfortable and stable on your feet. Tennis shoes are a good example.

Wear Comfortable And Loose Clothing

Restrictive clothing isn't ideal for Tai Chi as it will make you feel uncomfortable and it will restrict your movements. Instead, go for loose clothing that you feel comfortable in. Make sure you don't wear thick fabric if the weather is warm - you need to make sure that you're able to immerse yourself in your Tai Chi completely, without one part of your mind distracted because you're too hot or too cold.

Yoga pants and a loose t-shirt are a good idea, or loose fitting pants and a sports top. As long as you feel comfortable and your movements aren't restricted in any way, you're good to go.

During your Tai Chi, you should not be mindful of your clothing at all. That's the easiest way to describe what you should be wearing.

Ensure You're Hydrated But Not Full

It's important to make sure that you're hydrated before you start your Tai Chi practice. Remember this is a form of exercise as much as anything else and you need to be hydrated in order to focus and be comfortable. However, don't drink water too fast before you begin as that will simply give you stomach discomfort.

It's important to avoid eating a heavy meal in the hour or so before you start your Tai Chi. This will lay heavily in your stomach and cause you to feel sluggish and unable to concentrate. Instead, eat a light meal two hours or more before your Tai Chi and then eat a healthy, energy-rich meal afterward.

Keep a Tai Chi Journal

We know that there are many benefits to Tai Chi but at first you may not notice the small amount of headway you're making. Many people are put off when they don't notice major effects coming their way, but keeping a journal can open your eyes to the small pieces of improvement and benefit you're experiencing, before the major changes come your way.

You don't need to write large paragraphs and you don't have to write in your journal daily. Simply note down any changes you notice, such as more energy or a run of nights when you had good sleep.

Look back over your journal regularly and you'll be able to use it as motivation to keep going.

Fill Your Mind With Tai Chi History

We talked earlier about understanding Tai Chi's roots and history so you're able to understand what you're doing more effectively. This is a very important part of preparing for your first Tai Chi practice, but you shouldn't expect to be able to absorb everything before your first session.

Make it your aim to know as much as you can about Tai Chi's history, its foundations and its principles. That will help you to stay on track and understand more about what you're doing and why.

Do Some Research Into Movements First

Before you start your first Tai Chi session, it's a good idea to read about and watch popular Tai Chi movements. Later in this book, we're going to run through some of the best beginner movements to try but you might want to look these up on YouTube to see them in practice. That way, you'll know exactly what you need to do and you'll feel more confident in your first session.

Practice Breathing Exercises And Meditation

We're going to run through the key breathing exercise in a later chapter but for now, know that it's a good idea to practice these before you start your first Tai Chi session. Breathing exercises are ideal for many different situations, even to help you calm down when you're feeling angry or stressed during a day at work.

Turning your attention to your breath is a great way to ground yourself and feel in the moment. So, whenever you feel like your attention is drifting away, you can simply focus on your inhale and exhale, and pull yourself back to the here and now.

You might also like to get a head start on meditation. While Tai Chi doesn't require you to meditate in the way you might have in your mind, it does require you to focus your mind and push out any intrusive thoughts. We've already talked about the fact that many people struggle with meditation and feel put off trying endeavors like Tai Chi because of the perceived difficulty with meditation.

Try this exercise and you'll see how easy meditation can be if you put your mind to it.

- Sit somewhere comfortable, making sure that you're not going to be distracted
- Close your eyes and do a quick scan through your body to make sure that you're not feeling any discomfort in the way you're sitting or where you're sitting. If so, make the necessary adjustments
- Turn your attention to your breath. Notice how when you breathe in, your abdomen rises and when you exhale, it deflates
- Now, start to control your breathing. Breathe in for a slow count of five, pause for a second, and breathe out for another slow count of five
- Repeat this ten times
- If you notice any thoughts entering your mind, focus more intensely on your breath and push the thought away. Do not be tempted to analyze it in any way
- Once your ten breaths are over, sit quietly for a few seconds
- Notice any changes in how you feel. Do you feel more relaxed?
- Tell yourself that you're going to bring yourself back into the room. Slowly open your eyes and sit quietly for a few more seconds until you start to move.

That is a very simple meditation exercise that helps you to understand how simple it can be. Yes, there are many advanced meditation exercises that require visualization and almost trance-like concentration, but you're not going to be at that level and perhaps never will. It's also not required for Tai Chi.

By doing a little practice beforehand, you won't be as worried about distractions when you have your first Tai Chi session.

Tai Chi Is Not Just Movements, You Have To Use Your Brain!

A large part of Tai Chi is mental. You may see the movements and assume that moving your body means the whole practice is simply physical, but that's far from the case. We know that Tai Chi is known as 'moving meditation'. That means it has a physical and a mental side. By simply going through the motions with the movements, you might be moving your body and getting some exercise, but you're not getting the major benefits. In essence, you're not actually doing Tai Chi either.

With the use of key breathing exercises and imagery, the movements you perform will help you transcend stressful thoughts and feelings. Tai chi brings you firmly into the current moment and stops you from thinking about the past or jumping forward to the future. You're focused only on the breath you're taking, the movement, and the chi you're cultivating and allowing to flow.

While you don't do regular sit down meditation when you're practicing Tai Chi, you are using your mind to control not only your physical movements, but your thoughts too. We know that when moving your hands, you should imagine pushing against an invisible force, perhaps a gentle body of water. This helps to generate the desired amount of resistance to give you a good work out. However, in doing that, you're able to imagine the chi moving around your body. It gives you something to work with, without simply having to make do with the thought that chi is there.

Many people assume that to perform Tai Chi, you also need to use in-depth visualization exercises. That's not the case. Rather, you should focus on using imagery instead.

The key difference is that when you're using visualization, you're creating an image and you're immersing yourself into it to the point where you explore it. It takes you on a journey as you travel through the image and it moves and shifts as you do so. However, imagery is a little simpler as it means you're attaching a picture to a thought or feeling. That helps you to 'see' the invisible object and gives you motivation.

For instance, many people like to use imagery when thinking about chi. Obviously, you can't see chi, it's an invisible force, albeit a strong one. By attaching a color to it, you can see a stream of chi moving around your body, helping you to generate more because it will focus your mind increasingly.

It's a good idea to start with an exercise before you begin your Tai Chi practice. This will help you to relax and get you into the right mindset for your Tai Chi.

We know that Tai Chi has strong connections with nature, so to help you feel more grounded, try to imagine a beautiful, natural place that brings you calmness and joy.

Try this exercise:

- Sit down and focus on your breathing for a few minutes, until you feel your mind has calmed
- When you're ready, try to imagine a picture of one of your most favorite, natural places
- Try to really hone in on the details, including the weather
- Make sure the spot you choose is devoid of people or movement; you should only be able to see water moving or the wind blowing trees. The spot should also be gentle, i.e. no fast flowing water or high waves
- Stay with that picture for a while, really allowing it to fill your mind

- When you're ready to leave the image, tell yourself that you will be back soon, focus on your breathing before opening your eyes, and sit still for a few seconds before moving.

The idea of Tai Chi isn't to control your mind or force it into submission. It's about aligning your calmness with your thoughts. That means you should get to the point (not straight away) where you can hone in on calmness almost automatically. Your Tai Chi practice will, eventually, flick a switch that takes you from your busy life to a time when you can relax and rewind. It should feel natural and uncontrolled, but remember that you won't reach that point immediately.

What are Warm Ups And Cool Downs?

It's also important to remember that despite the calming nature of Tai Chi, it is still exercise. That means you need to warm up your body before you start moving and then cool down at the end. This will help to improve your practice and goes a long way to reducing the chances of injury.

Tai chi warm ups and cool downs are very similar to the types of movements you would do after a workout at the gym or a jogging session. It's about gentle stretches and encouraging circulation to the muscles.

Try this warm up routine before your Tai Chi practice, repeating every move five times on each side:

- Roll your wrists clockwise and anti clockwise
- Roll your shoulders backwards and then forwards
- Place one hand on the opposite shoulder and move that shoulder toward your opposite elbow. Repeat with the other arm
- Hold your arms out in front of you, palms facing downward and then upward

- Make your arms floppy and shake them
- Circle your hips one way, and then back the other way
- Complete a lunge with your left leg (keeping your knee soft)
- Complete a lunge with your right leg (keeping your knee soft)
- Move your legs to shoulder width apart and squat down, keeping your knees soft once more
- Circle your ankles one way and then back the other way
- Shake your whole body out to release tension

At this point, you should then practice some breathing exercises to get your mind in the right place before your Tai Chi begins.

A cool down routine after a Tai Chi session is quite easy to follow and generally includes stretches of all the main muscle groups.

It's important to keep any movement in the cooldown phase as slow and controlled as possible. Stretches should be gentle and shouldn't push beyond limits. You should also be sure to drink plenty of water after your practice to rehydrate - although Tai Chi seems gentle, you will still lose a lot of fluids during your practice.

- First, stretch out all the main muscles, e.g. the arms, legs, hips, and then move to circling joints, e.g. ankles and wrists
- Place one arm across your chest and hold with the opposite arm, feeling a slight pull on the back of the arm. Repeat with the other arm, a total of five times on each side
- Perform a lunge with your left leg for a total of five and repeat with the other leg for another five repetitions
- Move your legs to slightly larger than shoulder width apart and gently move into a squat, not dropping too far and keeping your knees soft
- Bend from the hip and lean your upper body to the left, feeling a slight stretch down the opposite side. Repeat on the other side - both sides, five times

- Slowly walk around the room in a circle, feeling your heart rate return to normal
- Finish off with some breathing exercises to maintain the feeling of calm.

Root Yourself

Learning how to root yourself is one of the most important parts of getting started with Tai Chi. This ensures that you bond yourself to the earth and draw stability and flexibility from it.

Imagine yourself as a large tree, with your roots burrowing far down into the ground. That is how a tree is able to stand up against the strongest wind and rain. By rooting yourself into the ground you're able to do the same, standing up against anything that life throws at you. It also reconnects you with nature and allows you to draw strength and chi from Mother Nature.

In essence, when you root yourself, your feet are strongly rooted to the ground and you feel like your body weight is sinking a little below the surface of the earth. By doing that, you generate power from your feet and it can move around your body, allowing chi to flow freely. At this point, your lower body is full and strong, but your upper body is loose and able to move freely.

When you are rooted, you're stable, balanced, and completely upright. Your posture is strong and your core muscles are engaged. That means your back is straight but relaxed. To achieve this position, your spine rests over your feet, sinking your entire central weight down into the ground. Try this and see if you can feel the bubbling of chi starting to move up from your lower body. It may take time to achieve this sensation but with the right amount of time practiced, you will feel strong and full of energy in this grounded position.

Developing a rooted position can be done in a few different ways.

You can practice by standing still in one position and holding it for increasingly longer periods of time. Start with two minutes, move up to five minutes, and see if you can hold it for longer as time goes on. The longer you can hold the position, the more you will be able to ground yourself to the earth.

Another option is to actually move your legs, but imagine that you're pulling your leg out of the earth, therefore pulling a root out and setting another one down. This builds energy and increases the sensation of being grounded.

- Stand with both legs straight, knees soft, and feet firmly planted into the ground
- Imagine your body weight sinking down, firmly grounding you into the earth
- After a short while, gently pull one leg up at the knee, pulling your 'roots' out of the ground. Notice the sensation and imagine that the root is visible underneath your foot
- Then, turn your attention to the other foot and feel your root on that foot growing stronger
- When moving your leg up, keep your body strong and still - do not allow your body to rise up as you move your legs as the will break the energy flow
- Repeat five times on each side.

When performing Tai Chi, always be mindful of your feet rooted in the ground when standing. This will help you to feel stronger and stable, while also allowing chi to flow up from the ground and around your body.

When you're rooted into the earth, you're able to move freely and in a flowing motion. That allows you to perform the movements associated with Tai Chi without jerking or allowing a break in the flow of chi.

Small Frame Vs Large Frame

When researching Tai Chi you will see different 'frame' styles and sizes. Generally, it's better to start with larger frames and then move to smaller frames as you become more experienced in Tai Chi.

Large frame movements are the basic movements in Tai Chi. These are predominantly found in the most common types, e.g. Wu, Chen, and Yang. In large frame movements, your movements are, as the name suggests, large and wide. You use more space and these are therefore easier to master because you don't have to be too intricate.

These types of movements are bold and large but they should still be controlled and flow freely from one to the next. The idea is that large frame movements help to strengthen the muscles, creating Jin. Joints are therefore loose and flexible, allowing you to move more freely and easily.

Imagine the body moving in large circular motions, flowing around itself and that's what large frame movements look like in a Tai Chi setting.

On the other hand, small frame Tai Chi movements are a little more intricate and therefore not considered suitable for beginners. However you will find them taught often in Sun style and sometimes in small frame Chen. The obvious difference here is that movements are smaller and don't take up as much space. Movements go around in smaller circles and the posture is higher up, with footwork that is more intricate and direct. In some situations, footwork is also more lively and less relaxed.

For anyone who is a little older or has mobility problems with the legs, small frame movements may be a little too demanding. In that case, you can understand why a large frame is a lot more common in health-related settings.

The best advice is to start with large frame movements and build your practice from there. In the future, when you feel confident and you've gained a lot of benefit from Tai Chi, you may like to experiment with small frame movements.

Points to Remember

- Ensuring you cover the basics will give you a better foundation on which to build your Tai Chi practice
- Stay hydrated before your practice and avoid eating heavy meals; eat at least 2 hours before your practice and eat an energy-rich meal afterward
- Choose the right time and place to begin Tai Chi, wearing comfortable clothes and suitable footwear
- A Tai Chi journal can help you notice small differences in your progress
- Practicing simple meditations before you start can give you confidence
- It's important to warm up and cool down when doing Tai Chi - it's still exercise!
- Rooting yourself is an important concept in Tai Chi. You ground yourself to the earth and draw chi from it
- Rooting also helps you to stand strong and maintain a good posture during Tai Chi practice
- Visualization and imagery are two subtly different things. Focus on imagery and attach images and colors to chi
- Large and small frame movements are common in Tai Chi
- Beginners should start with large frame movements as these are easier, less energetic and ideal for Tai Chi used for health
- Small frame movements are more energetic and take up less space
- You can try small frame movements after you have become experienced in large frame Tai Chi.

Chapter 4:
Getting Started With Some Key Tai Chi Movements

Now you know the key background information you need to understand Tai Chi, it's time to get practical.

The most important thing to remember is that you should not give up if you have a difficult experience the first few times. Tai chi is a practice that many people enjoy, but it takes time to master. Even the most basic movements may have you second guessing what you're about to do. Understand that practice makes perfect and simply go with it. Trying is better than doing nothing and before long, your confidence will grow, along with your ability.

You do not have to get it 100% correct to say you're practicing Tai Chi. Everyone has to begin somewhere and even the most experienced Tai Chi practitioners were once where you are now.

In this chapter, we're going to run through five of the key, basic principles to start with Tai Chi. Then, we're going to talk about some of the best movements for beginners. You can work through them in the same order we've outlined them, or you can choose the ones that call out to you.

However, remember that when practicing Tai Chi over the long-term, your movements will need to flow from one to the other, like water flowing from rivers into the ocean. The sequence we've outlined runs seamlessly from one to the other.

Key Principles

In order to begin practicing Tai Chi, you need to know the basic principles. These form the foundation on which you can build.

Earlier in the book, we talked about principles that form the basis for Tai Chi in terms of its background. However, these principles are related to the movements you make.

Practice them and understand them before you move on to any of the poses.

Principle 1 - Relaxation

You cannot practice Tai Chi correctly if your body is wound up in stress and anxiety. You need to do your best to relax your mind and body enough to move through the poses and therefore take advantage of the benefits.

Relaxation in the first principle on which all the others build. Without relaxation, Tai Chi won't work and the rest of the principles for movement will be useless.

In terms of Tai Chi, when you relax, you're allowing your body weight to sink into the ground. When we talked about rooting yourself in our last chapter, that's what you need to do in order to feel the energy start to flow and allow yourself to relax. However, with every single movement, you need to sink to relax.

It's important to see your weight being controlled by gravity; pinning it to the earth and keeping you steady. However, when we say 'sink', this doesn't mean slouching your weight down or allowing your weight to collapse. Instead, it means you're balanced, supported and using an energy that moves upward from the feet, to the top of the head.

To help you appreciate this, it's good to visualize water flowing up through a fountain, reaching a peak, and flowing back down again. That's how the energy is going to flow through your body; up from your feet, along your spine, to the top of your head, and spilling back down again. If you're struggling to understand how to sink your weight down, use this visualization exercise for a while before you start any Tai Chi movements.

When you see relaxation in this way, you'll appreciate that your body isn't rigid and it isn't slouched; the energy is flowing around you and you're grounded to the earth.

Principle 2 - An Upright Stance

We've talked about posture before and how it's important to be upright to allow energy to flow up and down the spine, nourishing all parts of the body. This is therefore one of the most important principles of Tai Chi when you start with the basic movements as a beginner.

The earth you are standing on is supporting you and feeling your weight. In Tai Chi, your weight is not only supported by the earth, but it belongs to it. It is simply a physical manifestation of the way in which gravity is holding your body to the planet.

To completely submit to relaxation, you not only need to imagine your feet sinking down into the earth, but you have to appreciate and feel the pull of gravity on your body. That way, you can relax because you know you're taken care of - gravity isn't going to let you down and you're not going to fall.

A key principle of Tai Chi movements is to align your body weight with gravity. That is how you achieve the correct posture for your movements. Imagine that you have a piece of string that extends a few centimeters above your head and an invisible force is gently pulling on it (gravity), keeping your head lifted and your shoulders back. Then, imagine that the string extends down through your body, running along your spine. There is a weight on the end of the string, which hangs a short distance below the bottom of your spine. That is pulling you down to the earth and keeping your feet planted firmly on the ground.

If you're someone who struggles with balance a little, this visualization exercise can help you to feel more steady on your feet before you begin Tai Chi. You can then go back to the visualization if you're struggling or feel unsteady at any point.

Put simply, when you're balanced, you're aligned with gravity, which allows you to perform Tai Chi movements.

Principle 3 - Weight Movement

You will quickly see that when you perform Tai Chi movements, you transfer weight from one leg to the other. This means that one foot is connected to the earth at all times, allowing you to remain steady, relaxed, and balanced.

For most people, the transfer of weight is the most demanding part of Tai Chi. It means that you need to be strong and steady at all times. This will improve with time if it's something you're struggling with, as your leg muscles strengthen with practice.

Many people assume that Tai Chi is all about the movements you make with your hands and while those are very important, it's best to focus on the basics first. That means how you steady yourself and root yourself to the ground. Then, you can use your hands with ease and not worry about balance or stability.

When you're rooted in this way, you can use the power from your hips and legs to help your hand and arm movements.

Principle 4 - Waist Flexibility

The ability to move from the waist is important in Tai Chi, meaning that you don't move your legs, you simply move your waist to help you complete the movements.

As with slouching, modern society has taught us that we move with our hands and twist however seems fit at the time. But, that often contributes to a large amount of tension in the body. When you learn to move from the waist, you remain strong and stable in your movements, whether completing Tai Chi or not. It also helps you to be rooted to the ground and as such, you can make the movements you need to make with definiteness and strength.

However, the important thing is to remember that three elements should be in a straight line at all times - the navel, the nose, and the eyes. When you move these three body parts should always be in alignment. You do not move your head and not your waist; your head and waist move together at the same time, to keep the line intact. That way, energy can flow freely and you're relaxed, allowing you to complete Tai Chi movements without the risk of injury or added stress to the body.

Earlier we mentioned imagining a piece of string run through your body, pulling your head up and your feet down to the ground. To that visualization, add the movement of your waist with your nose and navel all in alignment. At the same time, your eyes should follow the movement, aligning gravity, relaxation, and energy. When you do this, your upper and lower body are integrated and energy can flow.

Principle 5 - Fair Lady's Hand

This is another move that ensures your body is in alignment and you're not twisting unnecessarily or unnaturally. Again, this ensures the free flow of energy and allows you to relax.

Fair lady's hand relates to the way you move your arms. Your wrist should always be straight and in alignment with your elbow and the middle finger on that same hand. There should be no bending of the wrist away from the elbow - everything should be in a straight line. When you're making Tai Chi movements, the fair lady's hand is very important to ensure the cultivation and free flow of energy. It also ensures alignment within your body, with gravity and the earth.

However, your wrist should not be flexed or rigid, it should be soft to ensure that your entire arm is also relaxed. When you bend any part of your arm, e.g. your fingers or your wrist, you're creating a blockage and energy is unable to flow. Ensure everything is in a straight line, relaxed and soft.

These are the basic Tai Chi principles for movement. Each individual movement is a little different and will have its own set of guidelines but you should remember these five principles no matter what movement you are about to do. That way, you're always in alignment, energy can flow freely, you're relaxed, and you're not putting undue stress on any part of your body.

You'll also notice that you feel a lot stronger in your body and you will be much more stable when making movements. You should not wobble or become unbalanced when you follow these key principles.

18 Tai Chi Movements For Beginners

Up until this point, we've focused on readying yourself for your first Tai Chi session. We've also pushed home the fact that you may not find it so easy the first few times. Now it's time to put our words into action and show you a series of Tai Chi movements.

Below you will find a sequence to follow which covers 18 flowing movements. Remember that each movement should flow from one to the next. If you want to practice specific movements outside of your flow, that's entirely fine. That will allow you to master the technique before you go into the full sequence.

It's also possible that you may find a series of movements a little overwhelming at first. Again, that's fine. Stick to the first few movements in the series and slowly work your way up. However, in order to complete a full Tai Chi session, you should complete all 18 movements along with a warm up and cool down session.

Let's run through the whole sequence.

Warm up

Before you begin, be sure to complete some stretches to warm up your muscles and avoid injury. This will also give you more flexibility and movement as you go through the sequence.

For your warm up stretches, refer back to our warm up and cool down section earlier in the book.

Quiet Contemplation

Once you've warmed up, it's important to spend a few minutes in quiet contemplation. This sets the scene for your Tai Chi session and helps you to root yourself into the earth.

At this point, you could refer back to the visualization exercise we mentioned in our last section. Imagine the piece of string extending through your body, above your head and down to the earth. That will allow you to root your feet into the ground and stand tall.

At this point, quietly remind yourself of the need to stay in alignment at all times, e.g. your nose, navel and eyes, and your wrist, middle finger, and elbow.

Before you begin, you should remember that you will need to breathe through your nose the entire time if possible. This will help to calm your mind and avoid the stress reaction kicking in by breathing through your mouth or having your lips pursed.

We're going to talk about breathing exercises in our next chapter but for now, understand that you should focus your breath in your abdomen/stomach area and not the chest.

Remember that every moment should be slow and controlled. Every movement should also flow into the next without any pause. As you flow from movement to movement, remember to breathe.

Movement 1 - Commencing Form

This is the first movement in your sequence of Tai Chi movements.

- Stand tall with your legs apart, around shoulder width. Remember to keep your knees soft and not to overextend
- Raise your arms up in front of your body, stopping at shoulder height. Your fingers should be pointing downward, hanging in a relaxed manner
- Inhale and extend the movement by straightening your back a little more
- Slowly move the hands down, using the hand's heel first. As you move your hands down, exhale and picture yourself sinking into the ground.

Movement 2 - Broadening The Chest

This is an extension of the first movement.

- Flow back into the same starting position as the first movement
- Inhale and allow your arms to glide outwards, so your arms are at shoulder width, either side of you
- As you move your arms, picture your chest opening up and continue to breathe normally
- As you exhale, slowly move the warms back in front of your body and slowly down to your sides.

Movement 3 - Dancing With Rainbows

From broadening your chest, you will now slowly move into the next sequence, called 'dancing with rainbows.' This is one of the most commonly known Tai Chi movements and is often also incorporated into QiGong as a static posture. However, the difference here is that you will move in a flow, rather than standing still or holding position.

- Inhale and slowly transfer your weight onto your right leg. Bend your knee very slightly and at the same time, straighten the other leg
- Move your arms slowly over your head and allow them to float. Your right arm should curl over your head, so your fingertips move to your left ear
- Your left arm slowly moves down to the side as you turn your head to look at your left palm
- Inhale and transfer your body weight onto the left leg, bending the knee and repeating the process on the other side. As you do so your arm will make an image of a rainbow with the movement.

Movement 4 - Circling The Arms

Flowing from the last movement into this one should be simple as you slowly bring both arms back down to the side on the exhale.

- Inhale and bring both arms in front of you
- Cross your wrists and make sure your palms are facing up
- Raise your hands up toward the ceiling and over your head
- Move your hands apart and then slowly move your hands back downward, with the palm facing outward. Breathe out on the downward movement.

166

Movement 5 - Waist Rotation And Swinging Arms

When performing this movement, remember that twisting from the waist means keeping your navel, nose, and eyes in alignment at all times.

- Return to a central standing position and slowly raise your left arm in front of the body with the palm facing upward
- Your right hand should move slowly behind you at hip height, with your thumb pointing at the wall/scenery behind you
- As you move your hand, feel the hand scooping up all the fresh air
- Breathe in and twist slowly toward the hand behind you, moving your palm upward as you do so
- Slowly turn back to your standing position with both arms by your sides
- Repeat the same exercise on the other arm.

Movement 6 - Rowing The Boat

This movement is designed to give you a stretch across the chest area, but only move in slow and measured movements. It's tempting to allow the momentum to allow speed to gather, but keep everything slow and controlled.

- Stand with your arms by your side and then slowly raise them both by your sides, outstretched at shoulder/chest height - as far as is comfortable for you
- Your palms should be facing outwards and your thumbs should be pointing backward
- Slowly start to rotate your arms in large, anti-clockwise circles
- When you reach the top of the rotation, breathe out and allow your palms to face down to the ground.

Movement 7 - Hold The Ball

This movement involves some imagery as you need to imagine you're holding a ball or a balloon in your hand and you want it to move away from your hand, up toward the sky.

- Stand with your legs rooted to the ground and slowly raise your right arm, with the palm facing upward
- Watch your arm as you move it and picture a ball or balloon in your hand
- Slowly turn the palm downward and picture the ball or balloon gliding down and bounding back up
- As you raise your arm, you can lift your heel off the ground (the same side as the arm raised), to help you feel more comfortable
- Change sides and repeat the movement.

Movement 8 - Carrying The Moon

Carrying The Moon is a natural progression from the last movement as it also involves a similar movement and type of imagery. You can use the same image from the last movement if it helps to keep your chain of concentration intact.

- Stand with your legs rooted down the ground and raise both arms in front of you
- Picture a ball or balloon in-between both hands, with palms facing inward
- Twist at the waist and turn both hands to the left, turning your upper body in alignment as far as you are comfortable to go
- Avoid twisting your knee too much by raising the opposite heel off the floor
- Bring the ball down in alignment with your navel, continuing to keep both hands close together and arms straight

- Inhale and slowly move the imaginary ball or balloon to the opposite side.

Movement 9 - Twisting Waist and Palm Push

This movement requires a careful twist of the waist and is a little more demanding than the others. As we move through the sequence, movements will require more of a stretch. However, remember to work within your limitations and don't push your body too far if any stretch feels uncomfortable.

- Stand with your legs shoulder-width apart and pull your right arm back behind you, with the elbow bent, almost if you're taking back something you had offered someone with an outstretched hand. Your palm should be loose and facing upward
- On the exhale, slowly push your left arm forward with your palm upward and flexed
- Make small circles with the hand, pulling your hand into a fist (loose)
- Slowly pull the outstretched arm back inward and push the pulled back arm to the neutral position
- As you make the moment, your waist will slightly rotate to accommodate the movement.

Movement 10 - Cloud Hands

This is another famous movement in Tai Chi which is found in many different types.

- Stand with your legs shoulder-width apart
- Sweep your right arm toward the left, in front of your navel, with palms facing upward and relaxed
- Sweep your left arm up to the right, in line with your face, with your palm facing upward and relaxed
- Your movement should now look like a disjointed hug

- Inhale and gently turn your body at the waist to the right, gazing at the hand close to your face
- Slowly change your hand positions to the opposite sides, e.g. your left hand is now down by your navel and your right hand is level with your face
- Inhale and rotate at the waist to face your right hand
- You can gently lift your heels off the floor as you turn if it makes you more comfortable and keeps the flow smooth.

Movement 11 - Scooping The Sea

This movement is the first that requires repetition. You will repeat this exercise six times before moving onto the next one.

- Stand with your legs together and slowly step your left left forward (akin to a lunge stretch)
- As you do so, raise your arms in a scoop-like motion and bring your hands (palms up) in front of your knee, with palms crossed
- Slowly lift the heel of the right leg to make your movement smoother and more comfortable
- Slowly raise your arms upward, extending the scooping motion and then when they reach the top, separate your palms and slowly scoop them back down to your sides
- Transfer your weight back onto the right leg and repeat six times.

Movement 12 - Pushing & Pulling The Wave

This movement is similar to cloud hands but uses the legs a little more. This is another movement that requires repetition.

- Stand with your legs together and then slowly step your right leg forward into a lunge (bow stance)

- Slowly pull your elbows in toward your rib cage, keeping your arms and wrists straight and allowing your fingers to relax and hang down (palm facing downward)
- On the exhale, imagine that you are pushing a wave away from you, keeping the movement gentle and deliberate, not forceful
- On the inhale, imagine you are pulling the wave back toward you, so your elbows move back beside your rib cage
- This movement should feel like a rocking sensation and as you push and pull, be sure to transfer the weight onto your back leg (left leg). You should also lift the toe of the right leg as you transfer your weight back.
- Repeat six times.

Movement 13 - Spreading Wings

The mid-section of this Tai Chi sequence uses the bow stance a lot, which is a little like a lunge stretch. It's important to transfer your weight from front leg to back leg when moving, to ensure stability and comfort.

- Stand with your legs together and slowly step forward into with your right leg (lunge/bow stance)
- Slowly rock your body back, so that your weight transfers onto your left leg (behind you)
- As you do so, move your arms out at your sides, like wings. Your elbows should be slightly below your shoulders
- On the exhale, bring your arms together with palms in front and curl your fingers in toward you
- On the inhale, slowly move your arms back out by your sides, creating your wings once more
- Repeat six times.

Movement 14 - Straight Punch

This movement shows you Tai Chi's roots in martial arts. Remember to keep movements calm and controlled; you do not need to do explosive movements here.

- Stand with your legs slightly apart, knees soft and weight rooted into the ground
- Allow one arm to rest by your waist, creating a loose fist with your palm facing upwards
- With your other arm, on the exhale, slowly punch outward, with a loose fist
- Circle the hand a little before pulling your arm back to starting position on the inhale
- Swap hand positions and punch outward with the other hand on your next exhale
- As you move from arm to arm, you should feel your waist rotating slowly; remember to move your upper body in line with your waist
- Repeat six times on each side.

Movement 15 - Flying Wild Goose

Flying wild goose is another movement that requires control and smoothness. Move at your own pace and don't allow the movements to push the speed up. Remember, Tai Chi is deliberately slow.

- Stand with your legs together, knees bent and feet rooted to the ground
- Feel your arms sinking down toward the floor on your exhale
- As you inhale, slowly raise your arms out to your side, creating wings
- Slowly raise your weight up onto the balls of both feet as you extend your wings
- Sink back down to the ground as you lower your wings

- Repeat six times.

Movement 16 - Spinning Wheel

The spinning wheel is a series of arm rotations that energize yet relax at the same time. Remember to lift your heels from the floor if you need to as you raise your arms. This reduces undue stretching and helps you feel more stable and comfortable.

- Stand with your legs together, knees soft, and feet grounded
- Allow your arms to hang by your sides, bringing your palms inward, facing your legs
- On the inhale, bring both arms up and create a circle motion toward your right side
- As your arms reach the top, exhale and inhale again as they begin their incline once more
- Repeat six times before swapping arms and repeating on the other side.

Movement 17 - Bouncing Ball

This is the second to last movement, so make sure that you are mindful of the fact that your sequence is about to end, therefore slowing things down a little more.

- Stand with your legs just very slightly apart, knees soft, and feet grounded
- On the inhale, slowly lift your left knee in line with your hip and your right arm to rest in front of you at shoulder height
- On the exhale, return your arm and leg to standing
- On the inhale, lift your right knee in line with your hip and your left arm to shoulder height in front of you
- Remember to transfer your weight accordingly
- Repeat six times.

173

Movement 18 - Palm Presses

The final movement in this Tai Chi sequence is a gentle and relaxing movement. Be mindful that after this movement, you will go into the cool down sequence. This movement should quieten the mind and soften your body before ending your Tai Chi practice for the day.

- Stand with your legs just slightly apart, knees soft, and feet rooted to the ground
- On the inhale, raise your arms in front of your stomach, with your palms facing upward
- On the exhale, turn your palms to face downward and move your arms down, just below your navel
- Stay with this movement and repeat as many times as you need to, to end your Tai Chi practice.

Cool Down

Now your Tai Chi sequence is often, it's important to stretch your muscles and calm the mind before going about your daily business. Earlier in our book we talked about how to cool down, from stretching to gently walking around the room. You can also try some breathing exercises (in our next chapter), to help you to remain calm and relaxed as your practice ends.

Now can you see how relaxing Tai Chi can be? It's very easy to misunderstand Tai Chi and assume that it is extremely difficult to follow but this sequence should show you that's not the case. However, do remember that you're not going to follow the sequence off the top of your head immediately - you will need to refer back to this guide and you may even need to practice some of the moves before you put them together in a sequence.

All of that is perfectly normal and dedicating time and effort to this cause will help you to master the movements before putting them together and benefiting from the sequence.

However, if you need a visual introduction, you can always check videos of the movements on YouTube. This will help you to understand the movement while also reading the instructions.

Points to Remember

- When you first start Tai Chi, you will probably need to check back over the instructions as you perform the movement. All of this is normal
- The five key, basic principles of Tai Chi are: relaxation, an upright stance, weight movement, waist flexibility, and fair lady's hand
- Tai chi movements need to flow from one to the other. While you can practice movements individually, the whole sequence needs to be put together eventually
- To relax, you need to sink your body into the ground, aligning with gravity and feeling stable
- Moving at the waist means your upper body always remains in alignment. This is important when completing Tai Chi movements
- Transferring your weight carefully from one leg to the other means rooting. That way, your upper body is stable and movements are always smooth and slow
- Fair lady's hand describes how your elbow, wrist, and middle finger of each hand should always remain in a straight line, albeit it soft and relaxed. This helps you to make the right type of movement
- When following a sequence of Tai Chi movements you should always remember to warm up, spend some time in quiet contemplation, and cool down afterward.

Chapter 5:
The Breath, Your Forgotten Superpower

We know that Tai Chi is a form of moving meditation. While you do not sit down and meditate in the way you would imagine, it is an exercise that forces you to turn your attention inward, rather than constantly looking around you and becoming distracted with what is going on in the world.

Whenever you are in a stressful situation in life, or you simply feel angry or annoyed about something, there is one thing you have at your disposal that will always calm you down and bring you back to the here and now. Your breath.

Your breath never leaves you. From the moment you're born to the moment you die, your breath is the one constant that will always be there. We tend to take this bodily function for granted and we don't realize we're actually breathing most of the time. However, taking the time to become aware of your breath gives you a major tool at your disposal.

It's very easy to calm your emotions by grounding yourself with your breath. In Tai Chi, breath is very important. In our last chapter, we talked about the basic movements you can use to start with Tai Chi. You will see in the instructions that we told you what movement to make on your inhale and exhale. That information is important because it helps you to make the most of your movements while ensuring that your mind is in the right place.

In this chapter, we're going to talk about your breath. There are many useful breathing exercises you can do to help you focus your mind while also giving you extra athletic ability. When performing Tai Chi movements, you will find that moving on an inhale and exhale will give you extra flexibility and allow you to move a little further. When you perform specific breathing exercises, they will help you to feel less static and help your movements to flow.

Of course, your breath is also part of nature. It's a part of you, but oxygen comes from the environment around you and when you use your breath in the right way, you're grounding yourself and tapping into the cultivation of chi to another level.

Why Breathing Is Way More Than Just Getting Oxygen

It's not possible to perform Tai Chi correctly without breathing correctly. You might assume there is no wrong and right way to breathe but without breathing from the right place, you're not maximizing your lung capacity or the amount of oxygen making its way into your body.

Tai chi focuses upon the internal. While you're certainly benefiting your physical form, e.g. toning muscles, the predominant benefit is on the inside. You're cultivating chi and allowing it to flow around your organs. You're helping to store all-important life energy inside of you. Proper breathing techniques allow you to do that.

In Tai Chi, breath is considered to be akin to the opening and closing of a door. When you breathe in, you're opening the door, allowing energy in. When you breathe out, you're closing the door, pushing old energy and negative thoughts out. You can also think of your breath in terms of an arrow being pulled back on a bow and released. Find a visualization that helps you to picture your breath and whenever you feel stressed or upset about something, go back to that image.

This is a very powerful tool for dealing with life's ups and downs, not only for use when practicing Tai Chi.

Your inhale helps you to store chi and your exhale helps you to deliver chi where it needs to go. That is why it is important to make the correct movements on an inhale and exhale. For instance, in any Tai Chi movement that requires you to move your hands up and down, you would inhale when you move your hands upward. This means you're cultivating and storing chi. When you bring your hands down, you're exhaling and therefore delivering the chi to where it needs to go.

If you're ever confused about which movements to pair with an inhale and exhale, use that rationale to decide what to do.

Throughout our busy and stressful lives, we've all learned how to breathe incorrectly. We tend to breathe from our chests and that means that breathing form is shallow and fast. This is part of the 'fight or flight' response to stress. For that reason, when you become upset about something, you may feel like you're struggling to get enough oxygen in when you inhale.

Chest breathing doesn't allow you to maximize the amount of oxygen entering your lungs. Instead, you need to learn to breathe from your diaphragm, toward your abdomen. Later in this chapter, we're going to talk about diaphragmatic breathing and how to do it. For now, turn your attention to your breathing and try to pinpoint where you naturally breathe from.

If your chest is rising and falling, you're chest breathing. However, if your lower stomach and abdomen are rising and falling, you're already breathing from your diaphragm. This means you're getting a good amount of oxygen into your body on every inhale and you're maximizing the carbon dioxide you're exhaling too.

To breathe naturally, it's important to do so in a calm and loose manner. That means you're not tense, you're not holding your body rigid, and your breathing is free and easy. You should not be gasping for breath or feeling like you can't get enough air in. If that's the case, you need to focus on relaxation to calm your body. You should then notice that your breathing becomes easier and more natural.

Expanding The Capacity Of Your Lung

Any type of exercise, be it something gentle or more aerobic, requires you to expand your lungs to their maximum capacity and then allow them to deflate. This is the basic function of your respiratory system. By breathing correctly and allowing as much air to enter your lungs as possible, you're maximizing the amount of chi you have flowing through your body and you're giving your muscles the energy they need to help you move more freely and a little further.

We can take yoga as a good example here. When you first move into a pose, it will feel a little rigid and perhaps a little uncomfortable. However, your instructor will then tell you to make sure that you're breathing and not holding your breath. They will tell you when to inhale and exhale. You'll then notice that you're able to push the pose a little further and settle into it more easily. Tai chi is the same, except for the fact that you're always moving.

Breath is extremely important. It doesn't only keep us alive, but it allows us to reconnect with our emotions, calm down, cultivate and allow chi to flow, and increase our ability to move more freely.

For that reason, it's useful to learn how to maximize your lung capacity. This is the amount of air that your lungs are able to store at any one time. It's normal for lung capacity to decrease a little as we become older, and this can begin as early as our late 20's. When you exercise regularly, you'll naturally have a larger lung capacity, compared to someone who doesn't exercise as much, or at all.

Lung capacity can also be affected by certain health conditions. For instance, COPD (Chronic Obstructive Pulmonary Disease) affects the lungs and can reduce the amount of air this important organ is able to hold. As a result, a person with COPD may experience shortness of breath when doing very light activities.

While the lungs aren't made of muscle, you can picture them as such if it helps you to work out how to increase your lung capacity. When you work out, your muscles become stronger. You start off with quite weak muscles, but the more you work on them, the stronger they become, the more defined, and they help you to feel stronger and increase the amount of work you can do. You should think of your lungs in the same way. This will help you to focus on your Tai Chi movements without feeling short of breath and it will help you to reconnect with your breathing as you turn your attention inward.

To increase your lung capacity, there are several exercises you can do. You will need to do these regularly to see a major difference, but over a short amount of time you should notice that you become less breathless on exertion.

Let's take a look at a few ways you can work to increase your lung capacity.

Diaphragmatic Breathing

We mentioned diaphragmatic breathing briefly in our last section. This is sometimes known informally as 'breathing from the belly' because, in essence, that's what it feels like. Your diaphragm is a muscle just below your lungs, toward your stomach. When you breathe diaphragmatically, your lower stomach will rise and fall, rather than your chest.

This type of breathing helps to maximize lung capacity because there is more space for air to enter. It's also a deeper type of breathing which is very effective at helping you to calm down in difficult situations. All you need to do is focus on your breathing and picture the air entering your lungs and then exiting as you breathe out. Some people find it useful to picture breath as a color.

The diaphragm is part of the respiratory system and because it is a muscle, it can be strengthened with use and practice. Breathing in this way is considered to be the 'correct' way to breathe, because this muscle is supposed to do all the hard work in the process of breathing in and out. We've simply become so accustomed to using our chest, we've programmed ourselves to breathe in a different way. However, going back to basics isn't that hard.

- Sit or stand in a comfortable position, making sure that you're relaxed and settled
- Place one hand on your chest and the other one should sit just above your navel
- Breathe in through your nose for a slow count of two
- As you do so, notice that the hand on your abdomen rises and the hand on your chest moves very little
- Exhale through your mouth, using pursed lips, for another slow count of two
- As you do this, use the hand on your abdomen to apply a very small amount of pressure, therefore effectively pushing out the air
- Pause for a second and repeat as many times as you need

The more you practice diaphragmatic breathing, the more you'll start to do it naturally and therefore start to increase your lung capacity. This is also the best starting point for Tai Chi as it means that you're able to take in as much chi as possible during your movements.

Breathing Through Pursed Lips

Another breathing technique to help you to maximize your lung capacity is called breathing through pursed lips, or pursed lips breathing. This method helps to keep your breathing slow and steady, cutting down on how much work your lungs need to do to ensure your airways remain open.

By taking the pressure off the lungs, they're able to do what they need to do - function correctly and ensure the respiratory process of oxygen and carbon dioxide exchange takes place effectively.

- Breathe in through your nose slowly
- On the exhale, purse your lips and breathe out as slowly as you can. The process of breathing out through your lips should take longer than the inhale
- Repeat as many times as possible

To purse your lips, you simply make the movement as though you're about to blow on something hot. Again, the more you practice this type of breathing, the more you'll be able to slowly increase your lung capacity. Many people find this type of breathing a little easier to practice than diaphragmatic breathing but these methods can be done interchangeably to help you get the most out of your lung capacity as possible.

Of course, it's also a good idea to look for some general tips to help keep your lungs strong and healthy. This will ensure that they're working to capacity. When you use these tips in conjunction with the above two breathing exercises, you'll strengthen your lungs and ensure that you're able to take in more oxygen and chi during your Tai Chi sessions, and beyond.

- Avoid smoking. If you currently smoke, do your best to stop. You should also try to reduce the amount of time you spend in smoky environments, e.g. around people who smoke
- Fill your diet with antioxidant-rich foods, such as potatoes, broccoli, and carrots. Generally, bright-colored foods tend to have a high antioxidant content
- Exercise regularly

- Ensure that you're up to date with health checks and vaccinations to protect against flu and pneumonia
- Improve the quality of air in your home. You can do this by using an air purifier, cleaning regularly to get rid of dust and mold, and avoiding artificial fragrances.

You will not improve your lung capacity overnight, but with a little time, you will see improvement.

Breathing Exercises To Improve Your Tai Chi Practice

You can work on improving your lung capacity and using your breath to help you in stressful situations at any time. During your Tai Chi sessions, there are certain breathing exercises that will really help you to turn your attention inward and focus on the cultivation and flow of chi during your movements.

In this section, we're going to look at specific breathing exercises you can use to take your Tai Chi efforts to another level. Work on each one simultaneously if you prefer, or you can focus on just one and master that, before moving onto another - however, some do require a little extra experience and will need to be built up to.

All of these exercises are very beneficial and can be done anywhere, at any time.

Normal Abdominal Breathing

This type of breathing is also known as Zheng Fu Hu Xi.

Normal abdominal breathing is your general starting point for proper breathing. We talked about diaphragmatic breathing and that's very similar to this type of breathing once more. If you practice this method of breathing over the months, you will automatically breathe this way, therefore ensuring proper posture, good lung capacity, and the free flow of chi.

- Stand with your back straight
- Place both hands just below your navel, at the dan tian. Do not press down, you simply need to be able to feel the rise and fall of the area as you inhale and exhale
- Place the tip of your tongue on the roof of your mouth. This is done to connect yin and yang, therefore allowing balance and harmony
- Breathe in through your nose and feel your lower abdominal muscles pushing outward
- As you breathe out, pull your abdominal muscles back in. You should also feel your pelvic floor muscles contracting (known as the huiyin cavity)
- Repeat several times.

It's a good idea to stick to this type of breathing for a few months before you move onto another exercise. That way you're able to effectively train your mind and body to use this new method without any thought.

Dan Tian Breathing

Dian Tian breathing is one of the most important methods of breathing in Tai Chi, because it draws energy and oxygen from an area of the body that is said to store energy, or chi. You'll hear dan tian also called dantian, but they're one and the same.

When translated, the word means 'elixir field', which means this is a part of the body where chi is rich and abundant. This part of the body is also useful when meditating. Many people turn their attention to this area, often known as the heart chakra, to help them focus and draw positive energy.

Dan Tian breathing is said to help improve chi power and therefore allow internal energy to flow. You can use dan tian breathing in your Tai Chi practice or you can simply do it whenever you feel the need to ground yourself and feel energized.

You can also try this type of breathing upright or when sitting - choose whatever option fits your needs at the time. However, you should always remember to keep your back straight regardless of whether you're sitting down or standing. Posture is very important in this type of breathing, as it is in all types of Tai Chi movements.

You will see similarities between dan tian breathing and diaphragmatic breathing.

To use dan tian breathing:

- Place your left hand on your abdomen, just above your navel
- Place your right hand just below your left hand
- Turn your attention toward the bottom of your abdomen, specifically your pelvic floor muscles
- Breathe in and feel the lower abdomen expanding. At the same time, feel your pelvic floor muscles loosen and relax. Your right hand will move outward slightly
- Breathe out and pull in your pelvic floor muscles and the muscles in the lower abdomen. Keep the rest of your stomach area as still as you can. It should feel as though your pelvic floor muscles are pulling up toward your navel
- Breathe in and relax those muscles a little, but not all the way
- Repeat several more times.

Dan tian breathing is great for relaxation but it's also a good way to strengthen the pelvic floor muscles and maintain good posture. When breathing from this area, you're also increasing the flow of chi. It's important to avoid holding your breath or feeling too tense;

185

you should contract your muscles a little but not to the point where it feels uncomfortable.

You may also like to use a visualization of the chi as you breathe in and out. You can picture it as a color, floating up and down as you inhale and exhale.

Reverse Abdominal Breathing

This type of breathing is also called Fan Fu Hu Xi, Ni Fu Hu Xi.

As the name suggests, this type of breathing is the opposite of normal abdominal breathing and it's important not to try and practice both types simultaneously. If you try and practice both in the same few days or months, you're just going to find it harder to stick to one. You need to train your mind and body and that doesn't mean confusing matters.

- Stand with your back straight, in a comfortable position
- Place both hands just below the navel once more, at the dan tian point
- Again, place the tip of your tongue to the roof of your mouth
- Breathe in and pull your abdomen inward, while also pulling in your pelvic floor muscles. Do not pull too much. This should be a tense sensation but not one that feels difficult or uncomfortable
- As you exhale, push the abdominal muscles outward, releasing the tension in the pelvic floor muscles
- Repeat several times.

Reverse abdominal breathing won't feel as natural as normal abdominal breathing. That's because you're literally doing the opposite to what you've been taught to do for so long. However, once you practice for a while, you'll find that you're able to switch between the two.

It's possible that when you're practicing reverse abdominal breathing, the dan tian area may feel a little uptight or tense. If this happens, go a little easy and go back to your regular type of breathing, e.g. normal abdominal breathing. You may also find that if you gently rub or massage the dan tian area, the tension ebbs away.

Yongquan Breathing

Yongquan breathing is also known as Yongquan Hu Xi breathing or sole breathing.

Yongquan breathing requires a different stance to the other breathing exercises we've talked about so far. It is also a slightly more complex breathing exercise again, so it's worthwhile exploring the exercises we've talked about so far first, and then move toward this one.

- Stand with your legs shoulder-width apart
- Place your hands just below the navel, at the dan tian area
- Place the tip of your tongue to the roof of your mouth
- Breathe in and visualize chi moving down to the lower dan tian. Your abdominal muscles should expand as you breathe in, as you would do with normal abdominal breathing
- As you exhale, move your body down very slightly into a squat and visualize your feet sinking down into the ground. Your abdominal muscles should release on this exhalation. When visualizing your feet rooting, make sure that your vision goes below the feet by a short distance. This will ensure that chi flows deeply
- Once you have finished practicing this type of breathing, lift your heels from the ground and then place them back down and lift your toes a few times. This will allow chi to flow back through your body.

187

Another variation of this type of breathing is to twist as you breathe in and out. As you inhale, twist your body slightly to one side, making sure that you stay in alignment and don't break the straight line between your navel, nose, and eyes. When you exhale, repeat the movement by twisting to the other side.

Wuji Breathing

This type of breathing is also known as Wuji Hu Xi, or embryonic breathing. This type of breathing is a common practice in QiGong as well as Tai Chi.

Wuji breathing requires you to focus your mind on the lower portion of the dan tian, your main center of gravity and source of stability and grounding. You will need to use reverse abdominal breathing to use wuji breathing, so make sure you've mastered that before you move on.

- Stand with your back straight, in a comfortable stance
- Place both hands over your lower navel, i.e. the dan tian area
- As you breathe in, pull the abdomen in, along with the pelvic floor muscles. However, this time, also pull the lower back muscles inward
- Exhale and allow the abdominal muscles and pelvic floor muscles to relax, along with the lower back muscles.

Embryonic breathing is considered a slightly more complex type of breathing and it is designed to help you to cultivate and store chi at a higher level.

Laogong Breathing

This type of breathing is also known as Laogong Hu Xi breathing.

This is another complex type of breathing that requires visualization at the same time. The Laogong cavity is situated in the middle of your palms and you will need to visualize the chi moving to that particular area.

- Stand with your legs shoulder-width apart
- Place your hands below your navel, at the dan tian area
- Place the tip of your tongue to the roof of your mouth
- First, you need to practice embryonic breathing, by tensing your lower back muscles as your abdomen and pelvic floor muscles contract
- As you exhale, visualize that your hands are pushing chi downward - but do not move your hands at all. When you picture the chi moving, make sure that you see it a short distance below your hands.
- Repeat.

When some people practice this type of breathing, they feel a slight sensation on the palms of their hands. This could be a tingling, a warm sensation or even a cold sensation.

These breathing exercises may seem like too much to take in right now, but as with anything, practice makes perfect. You will get used to the different movements and visualizations you need to use as you inhale and exhale. However, make sure that you master dan tian breathing and normal abdominal breathing before you move on to any of the others.

After that, your next option should be reverse abdominal breathing. You will find that the more complex breathing exercises are based upon these types of breathing, giving you the knowledge to keep expanding your skill set.

Using Your Breath To Control Your Stress

A little earlier in this chapter, we talked about the fact that your breath can help you to calm down when you're experiencing heightened emotions.

There is a reason why a person who is experiencing a panic attack is told to sit down and breathe into a paper bag. That helps to slow down their breathing and focus their attention on a calming inhale and exhale motion.

When we become stressed, our bodies kick-start the fight or flight process. This means your body is preparing to fight a threat or run away from it. The problem with chronic stress is that a lot of the time, there is no real threat to fight or run away from. Regular, normal stress means that you're actually facing something that threatens your health or general wellbeing. These types of threats are short-lived and pass. However, chronic stress occurs when you're always in this state of alert, and as such, your mind is flooding your body with cortisone, the stress hormone.

A person experiencing chronic stress is at increased risk of severe health concerns, including heart disease. Cortisol increases the amount of inflammation in the body too, which also increases the chances of further illness. It's also important to remember that all of this places a major burden on your mental health and decreases your quality of life and generally happiness.

Dealing with stress isn't easy. It's not a case of simply talking about whatever is bothering you and then watching it disappear. There needs to be a strategy in place which uses several different tactics to overcome the problem. Stress can also ebb and flow, therefore returning once you thought you had the issue solved.

Tai chi is a very effective way to help reduce stress over the long-term. The breathing exercises we've talked about in this chapter can also be used at any time. You do not need to be practicing Tai Chi at that very moment; you can take yourself away to a quiet place and spend a few minutes focusing on normal abdominal breathing or dan tian breathing, and you'll have the same effect.

Your breath is a constant, as we've already explored. It grounds you in moments of extreme pressure and difficult emotions. A person who is angry and feels like they're seeing red can easily calm down by taking themselves away from the situation, closing their eyes, and focusing on their breathing.

Your breath is extremely powerful and by harnessing this power in the best way possible, you'll soon see that you can control stress without having to live a life feeling constantly overwhelmed.

When you use Tai Chi movements alongside regular breathing exercises, you'll notice that you become more mindful, calmer, and generally have a more serene outlook on the world.

Points to Remember

- Your breath is the one constant with you throughout your life that helps you to calm down, focus, and beat stress
- We often don't think about the fact we're breathing, but by turning your attention towards your breath, you can use it to direct chi and calm your emotions
- Your breath also connects you to nature because oxygen is a natural resource that moves throughout your body, nourishing your internal organs
- Using your breath at the right time allows you to push into movements a little more, therefore improving the benefits you gain
- It's not possible to perform Tai Chi correctly without inhaling and exhaling at the correct time

- Expanding your lung capacity can help you to avoid breathlessness and increase the amount of chi you cultivate, store, and allow to move throughout your body
- There are many different breathing techniques you can use, including diaphragmatic breathing, normal abdominal breathing, reverse abdominal breathing, and dan tian breathing, to name just a few
- Exercising, not smoking, cleaning up the air around you, and ensuring you consume a healthy diet full of antioxidants are all ways to boost your lung capacity
- The dan tian area is just below the navel and is considered the key pool of all chi. It is also known as the heart chakra
- Using your breath in stressful and difficult situations can help you to avoid acting out of character and can also help you to calm down during a panic attack.

Chapter 6:
Using Tai Chi To Still Your Mind

We know that Tai Chi is a form of moving meditation. We also know that many people struggle with the idea of meditation because they worry about not being able to quieten their mind completely.

As we have already established, there is no real need to completely block out any thought from entering your mind while meditating, especially while doing Tai Chi. You will be focused on the movements and your breathing, so it will be very difficult for any other thought to make itself known! However, it's still useful to understand how to try and quieten your mind as much as possible, therefore giving you a better chance of mastering this form of meditation.

In this chapter, we're going to reassure you about meditation once more and help you to understand how you can use imagery to keep your mind on track. We'll also give you some advice on how to avoid distractions. This information can be used outside of your Tai Chi practice too. If you often become distracted at work or you're prone to procrastination, much of this advice will help you to overcome this very common problem.

The Power of Imagery

When you are performing Tai Chi, your mind will be focused on what you are doing with your hands and body, and you'll also be using the correct breathing techniques to ensure that you're allowing chi to flow through the body without any blockages. However, it's also possible that from time to time, a thought will pop into your mind that insists on being heard.

This is likely to happen particularly at the beginning of your Tai Chi journey. As you become more experienced, you'll find it easier to push thoughts away, or simply pay them no heed and keep your mind on track.

It's important to remember that you do not have to empty your mind to use Tai Chi, or even meditation for that matter. If you assume that you need to empty your mind completely, you'll feel as though you have failed when a thought enters your mind and you can't seem to get rid of it. It's not realistic to assume this will happen.

Throughout the course of any day, whether you're concentrating or not, you'll have countless thoughts. Some of them are useful, some are a total waste of time and effort. However, the more you focus on them, the more space they take up in your mind, and the more important they will seem to you.

It's very normal to have intrusive thoughts from time to time. However, understanding the difference between a useful thought and a damaging thought is important. Many people who struggle with anxiety focus too much on thoughts that are unnecessary. It can sometimes be a worry or a fear that turns into a huge issue, simply because they focused on the thought too much

It's very easy to just say 'don't focus on it,' but we know that's almost impossible when you're struggling with anxiety anyway. What you need to do is learn how to ignore thoughts, rather than assuming that you need to block them out completely.

Imagery is a good way to do that.

Using imagery is a good tool for Tai Chi. We mentioned earlier that you do not need to use visualization and that there is a difference between that and imagery. When you visualize, you explore the scene in front of you. You picture yourself walking through it almost, picturing details and allowing it to play out. However, when you use imagery, you're simply attaching a picture or an image to something. You're not digging too deeply, you're just allowing yourself to see it more clearly because it has a color, a face, or a form.

Imagery can greatly improve your Tai Chi and can also help to focus your mind during your practice.

For instance, if you're struggling to get on board with the idea that chi is flowing through your body, you could give it a color. Purple is a good choice or perhaps silver. These are symbolic colors that have connections with spirituality. When you can see the color of chi flowing and growing, you'll be able to believe in it much more easily and as such, you'll focus on it more too.

We also talked about pushing your hands down or rooting your feet into the ground. You can picture roots emerging from the soles of your feet, delving deep into the earth and keeping you steady. You can picture a colorful cloud moving from your hands as you push them downward, and then draw it back up as you move your hands once more.

Imagery is a tool to make Tai Chi more accessible to all. Not everyone finds it easy to simply believe that chi is flowing. Some people need to have something they can really focus on. If that's you, imagery is a great way to really get deeper into Tai Chi and allow it to keep your mind on track.

If you're someone who does struggle with intrusive thoughts, e.g. worries and fears that occur during the day, there is one imagery exercise you can use to try and push them out of your mind. This can be used at any time, even if you're not trying breathing exercises or working with Tai Chi at that moment.

Try this:

- Acknowledge the thought that is bothering you

- Give it a color, perhaps black as it is a malignant thought that hurts you in some way
- Imagine a swirling, moving cloud of black in your hands, representing the thought that bothers you
- Take a deep breath in and on your exhale, picture yourself pushing that black cloud as far away as you can, using as much force as you can muster. You might also find it useful to say the word 'no' forcefully as you push
- Imagine the cloud is being pushed far, far into the distance, disappearing over the horizon
- Some people may find it useful to picture it being pushed into a chest, before the lid closes and the lock clicks shut.

This type of imagery experience is very useful for thoughts that aren't useful in everyday life. For instance, if you have a fear that manifests itself into intrusive and unhelpful thoughts, creating anxiety for you, this type of exercise may, over time, help you to handle it and push it from your mind for longer.

Do not expect it to go away the first time. You may need to keep practicing and imagining that thought being pushed away. It really depends on how persistent it is, but over time, it will dissipate. This means that you're using mind over matter, something which helps when you're practicing Tai Chi.

Imagery is something you can use in your everyday life, but when you're practicing Tai Chi, it's a good way to keep your mind on the task at hand.

Meditation in Motion

The regular type of meditation involves sitting down and turning your attention completely inward. It's something which many people struggle with and they often give up far too early, assuming that because they didn't master it the first or second time, it's not going to happen for them.

There is nobody on this earth that doesn't have the ability to mediate. It's simply a case of perseverance. Nobody is going to be able to sit down and get it right the first time. In fact, many would argue that there is no right or wrong way to meditate anyway. It's such a personal thing that it may require a personalized approach for you.

As a thought enters your mind, you simply need to avoid thinking about it or focusing on it. Just let it be. It may stay there, it may float away, but you do not need to analyze it. This will take practice, of course, because some thoughts are nagging. In that case, you can use the imagery we've just talked about to try and push it away. However, when meditating, it's far better to simply avoid placing too much thought or energy on anything that pops into your mind.

The fact that Tai Chi involves movement is a help. When you're moving, you're focusing on something. If you're sitting down, it's often easier to allow your mind to start ticking over. Before you know it, you've spent time analyzing your thoughts, rather than contemplating quietly.

A good way to see Tai Chi as meditation is through imagery, as we've already mentioned. When you're focusing on a color or a shape, you're meditating. It's as simple as that. Meditation doesn't have to include chanting or bells, it can simply be focusing on something at that very moment.

The main aim of meditation is to keep you in the present moment. When you start to meditate more deeply, it can also help you to find solutions to problems that have been persistent in your life. However, mindfulness meditation in particular is a very useful tool for anyone to use. It simply means that you're able to keep your attention right in this particular moment. You're not thinking back to the past and you're not worrying about the future. Both of these things cause stress if you do them too much. By living your life in the moment, you're able to make it as beautiful as possible and you're far less likely to live with regrets.

If you want to push your meditation a little further, you can try this walking meditation exercise. Make sure that you head off somewhere quiet and natural and do not go with anyone else. You need to be able to focus solely on what is around you, and that's going to be quite difficult if you're alongside another person. You should also turn your phone off, to stop it from distracting you as you try this meditation.

- Wherever you choose to go, spend a little time focusing on your breathing as you walk
- When you notice that your mind is calmer, turn your attention to the scene around you. You can continue walking if you want to, or you can stand still for a few moments. Some people find walking a little easier, as it requires a little less concentration
- Pick one detail in the scene around you. It could be the wind rustling the leaves in the trees or a dog running around in a nearby field. Whatever it is, make sure that you really zone in on it and pick out the small details. Explore the color of the leaves, the way the dog runs, or the way the wind whistles
- When you've exhausted all the small details of that particular object, choose another and repeat the process
- Keep going until you start to feel tired or enough time has passed. You should opt for at least 10 minutes to start, and try and build up the amount of time you spend in mindfulness meditation over a short while
- Once your walk is over, be mindful of the fact that you're going to end your meditation. Take some deep breaths and then return to your regular awareness.

While you were in this exercise, you were completely in that moment. You were focused on the small details going on around you, and you weren't thinking about anything else. That's what meditation is.

If you do notice a thought trying to make its way into your mind as you walk, you can simply push it away or just don't pay attention. The more you don't focus on it, the less important it seems, and its power diminishes.

It's very easy to assume that meditation is something that experts do. It's not the case. Anyone can meditate, they simply need to give themselves time to master it and feel like they're making progress. Even the most experienced people struggle sometimes; it often comes down to whatever is going in your day or how you feel at a particular time.

You may find that you can push all thoughts out of your mind one day, and the next you can't. That's because you have a lot going on and it's normal to feel a little overwhelmed. However, those are the days when you'll get the most benefit out of Tai Chi. In that case, schedule a quick Tai Chi session and see if that helps you to overcome those thoughts or feelings.

Remember, you need to make time for Tai Chi and don't assume that it's something you can keep putting off or canceling.

How to Deal With Distractions

Distractions are part and parcel of life. We live such hectic lives these days that it's normal to have so much going on that you can't concentrate occasionally. However, that doesn't mean it's something you should try and live with either.

When you first start Tai Chi, you may find that you feel distracted. You may feel a little silly doing these movements, or you might find that you can't shut off your mind and you keep remembering details of the day or things you need to do. Getting into the right mindset before you start Tai Chi is important and that's where breathing exercises come in.

Before you start Tai Chi, remember to spend some time in quiet contemplation, which also means focusing on your breath. The single biggest thing that will help you to avoid distraction is your breath. But that's not all.

We talked about imagery; that's another way to try and push away thoughts and stay focused. But, what else?

Time Management

Distractions often happen because we have so much to do and so little time. By organizing your time a little better, you may find that you feel calmer during the rest of the day, and you can therefore focus on Tai Chi and other things you need to do.

Procrastination is the biggest enemy most of us face in terms of productivity. We have so much to do that it simply seems overwhelming and as such, we put things off until tomorrow. The problem is, tomorrow you have twice as much to do and you're even more stressed. It's a vicious cycle that can often seem like there is no end to.

However, by managing your time, you will develop a more pragmatic approach and you'll be able to get more done, in less time.

There are several time management techniques you can try.

- **Prioritizing** - At the start of the day, write a list of all the things you need to do and then prioritize them in order of importance. Start with the most urgent or most important thing first and work your way down the list.

- **Scheduling** - Rather than simply adding a task to your ever-growing to-do list, you can schedule in a time to actually complete it. Open your diary and enter the task into a slot. Make sure that you schedule realistically however, otherwise you will simply overload yourself and cause procrastination to sneak in.
- **Eat the frog** - No, not literally! The eat the frog method simply means that the first task you complete is the one you don't want to do, or the one that is bothering you the most. By getting it out of the way (eating the frog), you're able to concentrate on everything else more freely. You're basically freeing up your mind.
- **Pomodoro technique** - The Pomodoro technique is a very popular option. This allows you to work in short bursts with regular breaks. Set a timer and work solidly, with total concentration, for 15 minutes. Take a 5 minute break and then set your timer for another 15 minutes. Do this five times and then take a longer break, up to half an hour. Repeat as many times as you need.

It's true that to-do lists simply don't work. Without prioritizing the tasks or scheduling them in to complete, you're just adding to an ever-growing list that seems very overwhelming when you look at it. As such, you ignore it or keep putting things off. That adds to the stress you're experiencing and you will find it harder and harder to find time for your Tai Chi.

Scheduling Tai Chi

If you're going to obtain the benefits of Tai Chi, you will need to make time for it. That means you need to practice it as much as possible. Two or three times per week is a good starting point, but anything you can manage is better than nothing.

However, you should also make sure that you schedule your Tai Chi in, and don't cancel it. Don't see Tai Chi as something that is optional, instead see it as something which you enjoy and something which enriches your life

If you see it as work or something you don't particularly have time for, it's not going to be very beneficial to you. However, when you learn to look forward to Tai Chi and you start to see the benefits coming your way, you'll notice that you actually enjoy what you're doing and you'll want to do it more.

Unless there is something extremely pressing that you cannot ignore, don't cancel your Tai Chi sessions.

Understand Your Limitations

One of the most important things to remember is that you're only human and therefore you have limits. It's easy to take on too much, something most of us are guilty of these days. When you do that, you become overwhelmed and stress finds it very easy to enter into the equation.

Be kind to yourself. You can only do so much and what you don't complete that day, you can easily do the next day. That doesn't mean you're procrastinating and putting things off; it means you appreciate that you're not superhuman.

Tai chi will help you to understand your limitations in life and it will help you to appreciate your own value. Tai chi should be something you choose to do for yourself and because you want to obtain the benefits it will give you. That isn't selfish, that's putting your own health and wellbeing first. When you do that, you're able to do everything else you need to do and enhance the lives of those around you.

Distractions are very easy to come by when you feel like you have to wear a million hats in life and you simply don't have the time to complete everything you feel you need to do. Rather than allowing that pressure to take hold of your life, understand that you can only do so much and be okay with it. It may feel odd at first, but over time you'll start to understand that whatever you're doing, it's more than enough.

Get Enough Sleep

Sleep is vitally important but something that we often put off or see as a luxury. If you're not well-rested, you're not going to be able to battle distractions and you won't find time to practice your Tai Chi. During your Tai Chi sessions, you'll also find it far easier for thoughts to make their way into your mind and you'll be so exhausted that you can't find the will to ignore them.

On average, adults need between 7-9 hours of sleep per night, but everyone will have their particular 'happy amount' between those hours. You should also make sure that your sleep is of high quality, i.e. you're not waking up often.

To help you get good quality sleep, follow these pieces of advice:

- Try to go to bed at the same time every night and wake up at the same time every morning. This will set your circadian rhythm (body clock) and help you get into a routine
- Avoid anything too stimulating before bed, i.e. action or horror movies, video games, or loud music
- Do not use your phone in the hour before you plan to sleep and if you need to, make sure that you set it to night mode. This will cut down on the amount of blue light your phone transmits, which can affect your circadian rhythm and trick your brain into thinking it's day time
- Avoid alcohol, coffee, or sugary drinks before bed. Instead have a warm, milky drink to relax you
- A warm bath before bed is a good idea, however do not have it too hot

- If you're going to work out, make sure you complete your workout at least three hours before you plan to sleep
- Avoid heavy meals in the hours before bed. If you must eat, make sure it's a light snack that isn't too fat-laden
- Make sure your bedroom temperature is comfortable. Open the window to increase ventilation and do not sleep with the heating on as this may cause you to feel 'stuffy'
- Remove any technology from the bedroom, including the TV
- Ensure that your sleeping area is comfortable. You could try a weighted blanket, as these have been shown to help increase sleep quality and comfort
- Check your pillows - if you've had your pillows for longer than six months, they may be losing their supportiveness and could cause aches and pains in your neck that make it hard to sleep
- Try a white noise machine or app. If you don't like these, you could run a fan in the background and focus on the noise.

These are all ways to try and work toward a better night's sleep on a regular basis. When you're well-rested, it's much easier to concentrate and distractions won't be such an issue. You'll also have more energy and feel more upbeat and positive.

Points to Remember

- Tai chi does not require you to completely quieten your mind and block anything from entering it. It simply asks you to pay no attention to thoughts and to concentrate on your practice
- Allow thoughts to float into your mind but do not pay them any attention. Simply let them be and eventually they will become less important and therefore disappear
- We live busy and hectic lives and it's very easy for thoughts to turn into fears and worries. This can cause anxiety. Tai

chi is a good way to manage those thoughts, but first you need to learn how to avoid them taking over your life

- Tai chi is a form of moving meditation and the fact that you're moving helps you to concentrate much better
- Imagery is very useful in Tai Chi practice. You can use it to give chi a color, therefore helping you to picture it in reality a little better. You can also use imagery to push away intrusive thoughts
- Everyone can use meditation. You may not find it useful the first few times, but with practice you'll find it easier and you'll notice benefits over time
- Distractions are a product of our busy lives. You can manage them with practice
- Mindfulness meditation is a useful way to stay in the here and now and avoid stress
- Managing your time better means you're less likely to procrastinate and therefore you won't struggle with distractions as much
- Tai chi is something you need to dedicate time to. Do not cancel your sessions - put everything into them and they will pay off.
- Making sure you get enough sleep is another way to stay on track and avoid feeling overwhelmed

Chapter 7:
How to Get The Most Out of your Tai Chi Practice

We're almost at the end of the book. How do you feel about Tai Chi now?

The hope is that you're keen to get started and begin noticing the benefits that this ancient practice brings to you. However, it's also important to remember that nothing in life comes easily. You have to dedicate yourself and really throw your all into Tai Chi for it to manifest the benefits you want.

It's also important to understand that Tai Chi is fun. Yes, we all want the benefits it brings, but if you can see it as something you enjoy, you'll be able to dedicate yourself to it far more easily. That way, you'll make time, you won't find it easy to cancel, and you might even encourage those around you to try themselves.

This final chapter is dedicated to ten useful tips that will help you get the most out of your Tai Chi practice. By following these tips in your everyday life, you'll notice that you start to feel more balanced and grounded in everything you do. Remember, Tai Chi is about movements and mindset, but it's something you can incorporate into every second of your day. You don't have to be doing the movements to cultivate chi and feel it flowing throughout your body.

Tip 1 - Remain Open And Curious

Tai chi is not something you always need to be completely serious about. Yes, it's something you need to take seriously, but having a serious mindset isn't necessary.

You can be curious and playful when it comes to Tai Chi. You can enjoy the process and see it as something that enhances your life, rather than something you have to do and work at. While you need to put forth the effort, you can be curious and learn more as you go through your journey.

There is so much to learn when it comes to Tai Chi. Even the most experienced individuals find new things to try and master regularly. From different styles to different movements, the options are endless. Find the excitement in that, rather than assuming that Tai Chi is a subject you must drag every single ounce of knowledge from.

You will not learn everything there is to know about Tai Chi in a lifetime. But, you can find great benefit from it and allow it to nourish your life, bringing a true sense of fulfillment and calm.

Keep learning but don't overstretch yourself before it's time. Focus on one thing, understand it and feel confident before you look to learn something else. Keep practicing the previous task while you look toward new knowledge. This will be something that nourishes your life and brings you great interest.

There is a lot to learn in terms of traditional Chinese medicine too. If you want to read into that side of things, you'll also find a huge amount of knowledge to be found. It's almost like a form of escapism once you see Tai Chi in the right way.

Remember, it's a hobby. It's something you do because you enjoy it and because it brings you health benefits. It's not a class you don't enjoy.

Tip 2 - Always Observe The Flow Of Nature

Nature is all around us. Every single second of the day, Mother Nature is working her magic. Much of the time, we don't even realize it or notice it.

You may be reading this book sitting next to a plant or flower of some kind. While you're reading, that plant or flower is growing, photosynthesizing, and living a life of its own. You're not even aware of it, and of how amazing every single thing around us really is.

If you want to enhance your Tai Chi practice, it's a good idea to become at one with nature. Don't simply allow it to happen around you, observe it and try to understand it. The more you see the natural world and open your eyes to its wonder, you can reconnect with the earth around you.

Remember, a huge part of Tai Chi is reconnecting with nature. If you can do that in your everyday life, you'll find it much easier when it comes to actually perfuming Tai Chi during your sessions.

If you're regularly practicing Tai Chi in the house or indoors generally, mix things up and head outdoors. You may find that you can concentrate more easily or you feel a surge in chi because you're in the fresh air and surrounded by the wonder of Mother Nature.

When you're outside on a walk or you're traveling to work, spend some time looking at the natural things around you. Become curious about how trees grow, or simply watch a cat as it stalks a mouse in a field. These are all natural practices that are part of the great circle of life and understanding it, or at least observing it, will help you to become more connected with nature and within yourself.

Tip 3 - Ground Yourself At All Time

We have already talked about grounding yourself in terms of roots. That means you use imagery to picture roots extending below the soles of your feet, far into the ground. This will give you stability when practicing Tai Chi and allows you to balance when performing the movements. However, you can use this in your everyday life too. When you do so, you'll enhance your Tai Chi because your balance and stability will improve greatly.

Throughout your everyday life, picture those roots. When you're sitting down during the evening, after a long day at work, place your feet flat on the floor and imagine those roots extending down. You don't have to be standing to do this and you don't necessarily need to be about to do Tai Chi either.

Grounding yourself in everyday life is useful because it helps you to recognize your connection with the earth. It allows you to feel calm and less stressed, and it gives you a sense of being completely protected by nature. You're also aware of gravity holding you to the ground, giving you a calm feeling of balance.

We talked about picturing a string running down your spine, extending above your head and below your tailbone. This is something you can visualize as you're going about your day. It will help you to ensure a good posture at all times and therefore help chi to run freely throughout your body.

Tip 4 - Experience Movements as a Whole

Every single part of your body moves independently. You have muscles, joints, bones, and ligaments that ensure your arms move independently to your body, your fingers move without moving your wrist, and your legs move without moving your upper body. The human body is complex and can move in all directions.

However, in Tai Chi it's important to recognize your body as a whole. While your legs may easily be able to move without the rest of your body, you should appreciate that for those legs to move, other parts need to tense, engage, and focus. Your brain sends signals to your leg muscles to get them to move when you're walking. This is a process that happens without conscious thinking on your part, but it's all going on behind the scenes.

Start recognizing the joint effort throughout your body for one single limb to move. See every movement as a whole, rather than individual parts. This is another way to ground you and bring a sense of wholeness throughout your life.

In Tai Chi, we've mentioned that movement should be from the waist and that you should move your upper body in alignment, keeping your navel, eyes and nose in a straight line. You could easily move your waist without doing that, but by doing so you're creating a blockage within your spine and chi isn't able to flow as easily.

Keeping everything in alignment means your body moves as a whole. Bringing your awareness to that fact will greatly improve your Tai Chi and allow chi to flow more freely.

Tip 5 - Never Stop Your Practice

It's easy to wonder why Tai Chi isn't becoming easier or why you're not noticing major benefits yet. The truth is that it's not going to happen overnight and that's something you need to be aware of. Practice is the key to Tai Chi.

Understand from the very start that without regular practice and effort, you will not improve and you probably won't see much benefit coming your way. That doesn't mean you need to practice every single day, but it does mean making the basics of Tai Chi part of your everyday life.

Focus on breathing correctly, fix your posture, become aware of nature all around you, and try to remain as grounded as possible. These are all ways you can practice the principles of Tai Chi without actually doing the movements. Then, when it is time to practice movements, you'll find they come easier to you and you're able to concentrate far more easily than otherwise.

Tai chi isn't easy. It's not something you're going to click your fingers and become good at. Nobody is a natural at this. However, you will improve greatly with time and effort. Dedicate yourself and look forward to what will surely come your way.

Tip 6 - Get Your Loved Ones Involved

It's not the best idea to involve people in your Tai Chi from the very start. Some people find it useful to be surrounded by other people, but many need a quiet and contemplative start to be able to find their feet and understand the workings behind this ancient art.

However, after a short while, you may find it beneficial to involve your loved ones. That way, they will understand what you're doing and they will be able to support you in your endeavors. They may even find that they want to do it themselves and look toward the benefits. In that case, you can support them and help them with what you have learned so far.

If you're someone who struggles with motivation, it may be that involving another person from the start is actually better for you. Remember, Tai Chi is a personal subject and while most people find it easier to focus on themselves at first, perhaps you need someone you can work alongside and therefore be held accountable to.

In that case, ask a friend or family member to try Tai Chi with you. You can learn from one another and motivate each other during those times when you're struggling or you simply don't feel like Tai

Chi is working for you - because there will be times like that at the start. It's important to push past moments like that and keep going. The results are just around the corner.

Tip 7 - Avoid Negativity & Forgive Your Day's Problems

Stress is one of the biggest problems in our society. We know that Tai Chi is a good way to manage stress and can help you to free yourself from chronic stressors in your life. However, that's not going to happen unless you try your best to avoid negativity generally.

Every day will have something negative within it. This is just a general part of life that we cannot completely escape. The key is to accept this and forgive the day's problems without allowing them to overtake your day and turn it wholly negative.

Whatever has happened during the day, forgive those problems. They may not be solved and they may continue into another day, but for now, forgive them and put a lid on them. You can use imagery here if it helps - picture the problem being put in a box, the lid being placed on top, and picture yourself feeling happier and lighter.

If you can learn to do that, you'll develop a more positive attitude overall. Problems come and go. For sure, some need extra attention and care, but you cannot allow them to railroad you into acting in negative ways that may become extremely damaging over the long-term.

Tai chi, as with all forms of traditional Chinese medicine, rely heavily upon mindset. You need to try and be as positive as possible and see life as something that happens around you, rather than you having to constantly try and shape it and put out fires. This also taps into mindfulness. When you can observe what is happening around you, you're more able to make sensible decisions, rather than jumping at the first thing you think makes sense. Much of the time, that's just a knee-jerk reaction that makes things worse.

Becoming more positive isn't easy if you have a negative mind, but it's something that you can practice over time. Use positive affirmations and reframing to help take negatives and turn them into positives.

Tip 8 - Balance Your Strengths And Weaknesses

One of the key principles of Tai Chi and other traditional Chinese medicine methods is the balancing of yin and yang. These are opposites which need to balance in order to restore harmony.

Every single person has positive traits and negative ones. We all have strengths and weaknesses. While you can work on your weaknesses and try and make them into positives, some would argue that it's much more fruitful to accept your strengths and weaknesses equally. This helps you to balance yin and yang and bring about a sense of harmony within you.

It's easy to become too focused on what you can do better, rather than celebrating the things you do well. This seems to be a human trait that we all fall foul of occasionally. However, when you focus on it too much, you lose balance. Your Tai Chi practice will benefit greatly from simply accepting both your strengths and your weaknesses and being okay with both sides.

You're human after all. You cannot be all good and you cannot be all bad. You're a balance of the both and keeping that balance even ensures that yin and yang are in total harmony within and around you.

Tip 9 - Try a Tai Chi Class

If you're struggling with Tai Chi and you're learning yourself, it may be a good option to reach out and find a local class. You can search online to find a class near to you. Social media is also a good place to find classes that specialize in the type of Tai Chi you want to focus on.

It may also be that you're doing well with your Tai Chi at home, but you want to push the boundaries a little and attend a class to see if you can learn in a different way. This is a good mindset to have because it means you're always curious about the practice and what you can do to increase the benefits that come your way.

There are many different classes out there, so you simply need to find one that suits your needs. Some classes are larger than others, or you may find online classes that allow you to remain in your home environment but still give you the social interaction you're seeking.

The truth is there is no set way to do Tai Chi. You can do it alone, you can do it with a loved one, you can find a stranger in the park and join their session, or you can take a class. If you want to, you can do a little of both. However you choose to do Tai Chi, the fact that you're trying is more than enough.

Tip 10 - Always Ask Questions

You're not going to learn everything there is to know about Tai Chi from this book. You're not going to learn everything there is to know about Tai Chi in a short time either. As we've mentioned before, there is a lot to discover and this is a journey, rather than a short sprint. As such, don't be afraid to reach out and ask questions about things you're unsure of or things you want to learn more about.

Join some social media groups about Tai Chi and interact with members. You could also attend a class and ask the instructor if you can ask some questions when they have some spare time. Connect with other group members and discuss your experiences together. There is so much to learn from other people who practice Tai Chi, simply because everyone's experience is so different.

Rather than not completely understanding something and just persevering, asking a question may help you overcome a block and keep moving forward to greater enlightenment. Remember, this is a totally new endeavor and asking questions means you're keen and ready to learn.

These ten tips are important if you want to push your Tai Chi to another level. The journey you're about to embark on may be truly life-changing for you and that means you need to dedicate yourself entirely. That being said, this shouldn't be something which seems like a huge effort or something which adds more pressure to your life. It should be something which feels free and easy.

All of the advice in this book is designed to make your journey a little clearer, but with every step you take, there may be questions or queries you need to explore. Push through those barriers and be brave enough to reach out and ask the people around you for advice. You can easily make Tai Chi a social event for you, as much as it is a health-related endeavor too.

Points to Remember

- Tai chi should be something you enjoy in order to really obtain the benefits
- There are many Tai Chi principles you can follow in your everyday life, which will enhance the quality of your Tai Chi sessions and movements
- It's important to be curious about Tai Chi and learn more
- Ground and root yourself even when you're not doing Tai Chi movements. This will help you to feel at one with the earth, increasing stability and balance

- Observe nature and its natural processes. By doing so, you'll ground yourself and connect with nature
- Your body moves as a whole. Even though individual parts move freely, your body is one and being aware of this helps you to feel grounded
- Involving your loved ones in Tai Chi may help you to feel motivated
- Do not allow the day's negativity to overshadow a positive mindset
- Practice is important if you want to improve and notice the benefits
- Being positive overall will help your Tai Chi practice
- Tai chi classes are a good way to interact with others who have the same interests as you
- Everyone has strengths and weaknesses. Balance yours in order to balance yin and yang within you
- Don't be afraid to ask questions if anything about Tai Chi confuses you - it's the only way to learn.

Conclusion

We're now at the end of our book and we hope that you're ready and raring to get started on your personal Tai Chi journey.

We've been through a lot together as we've moved through the pages in the book and the hope is that your confidence is raised and you're intrigued and even excited to try Tai Chi for yourself.

The benefits really speak for themselves. This is a practice that has been in existence for thousands of years; in truth, nobody is 100% sure just how many years we're talking about, but it's certainly many, many more years that we can comprehend. For that reason, you can have complete confidence in the process you're about to go through and what you're going to learn.

Many people go into Tai Chi for health benefits, but it's something you should enjoy and find fascinating too. Tai chi should become your passion and something you want to do, not something you feel obliged to do. If you ever start to feel that way, you need to change up your practice a little and take a new approach.

The great thing about Tai Chi is that it's a never-ending cycle. You will never learn everything there is to learn about it and then become bored. There will always be something new to come your way and something else you can try.

By connecting with other Tai Chi enthusiasts, you'll also form a social network that you can interact with. You'll learn from other people, they will learn from you, and you'll find a true sense of camaraderie as a result.

Tai Chi Can Be Your Answer to Stress

We know that Tai Chi has many health benefits but we can't ignore one of the biggest - stress reduction.

The world we live in is high pressure. We're always connected via the online world and we're never given the time we need to simply 'be.' In fact, we're taught to believe that if we relax, we're somehow being indulgent and wasting precious time.

The truth is that reconnecting with yourself is a priority in life and certainly not an indulgence. It's something we all need to feel grounded and calm. By practicing Tai Chi regularly, you'll notice that you don't feel as overwhelmed or stressed and that you have coping mechanisms in place for those times when your emotions do rise and fall.

The truth is that you're always going to experience a certain amount of stress in life. Tai chi is not going to wave a magic wand and take stress away from your life forever. It's not going to stop you from ever feeling overwhelmed, angry, or upset again. These are the things we need to face in life, however it will give you a very strong coping mechanism and a new mindset to face those challenges.

You'll feel more grounded, serene, and pragmatic about life. You'll have a greater understanding about the balance of yin and yang and you'll appreciate that positive and negative will always be around. You'll know that it's nothing to be concerned about as long as the balance remains equal.

Start With What Feels Right to You

So, what's your next step? There are several options in front of you. You can read the whole book through and then try the exercises that call out to you, or you can pick a specific section and work through that before moving onto the next.

How you start with Tai Chi is personal. There is no right or wrong answer here because we all work in different ways. That means we all learn in different ways.

The best advice is to start in the way that seems right to you. If you want to practice breathing exercises first, do that. If you want to try and understand how to root yourself and improve your posture before you do anything else, that's the right step for you.

What you shouldn't expect is to jump into the sequence of movements and expect to get it right the first time. You shouldn't expect to feel any different either. You will need to complete the sequence a few times before you notice a change in how you feel and you'll need to perform them with the breathing exercises. However, every small benefit is a win. If you complete a sequence and you feel more upbeat than when you started. You won that day and you'll win bigger the next.

What matters most is that you're trying and with that intention, you're showing the world around you that Tai Chi is something you believe can work for you.

Believe it.

One Last Thing Before You Go …

Your Tai Chi journey is just beginning and we hope that this book has given you all the information you need to get started. Remember, you need to continue learning and asking questions to take your journey from this initial point, to a more beneficial place in the future.

We're keen for you to get started on your own Tai Chi journey but before we do, we would like to ask you to do one thing for us.

We want to keep helping people around the world to discover subjects such as Tai Chi. The benefits are so far-reaching that more people need to understand this ancient art and feel confident enough to get started. However, for us to do that, we need you to help us reach as many people as possible.

219

To do that, you simply need to leave us a truly honest review of the book you've just spent time reading.

What parts of the book did you find the most helpful? Which exercises really called out to you and made you want to get started on your own journey? How do you feel about the journey in front of you right now? We're keen to learn more!

The truth is that many people don't bother to leave reviews; in fact, most people don't read a book to the end. The fact you have means you're different, you stand apart from the rest. We want to know what you thought about our book because your views matter to us.

It's worth remembering that most people read reviews before they choose whether to spend their money on something. The same goes for books. Perhaps you read reviews of this book before you decided to buy it and learn more about Tai Chi. When you leave us an honest review, you're helping other people gain the confidence to buy our book and then gain the same great knowledge you've learned in these pages.

When you think of it that way, you'll have a huge helping hand in allowing other people to discover the fantastic benefits of Tai Chi too, just like you have.

As authors, reviews are our life-line. They help us to keep writing content for people around the world and it's something we feel passionate about doing.

So, if you feel that this book has helped you to understand Tai Chi and it's given you the push of confidence you need to get started, we'd be so grateful if you could leave us a review. You don't need to write too much, just let other people know what you think. It also helps us to understand what you liked and what we might be able to do better. Feedback is good and it helps us to carry on writing these books for you. You can even let us know what you might like to learn about next.

Rest assured, we read all reviews so we will definitely see your comments and take them firmly on board.

Leaving a review is quick and easy and there are a few different ways to do it, depending on how you read the book.

If you listened to the book on Audible, you can leave a review by pressing the three dots in the top right hand corner of your screen. Then, you just need to click 'rate and review'. Let us know what you think and give us a star rating - whatever you think we deserve!

Maybe you're reading this book on an e-reader, maybe a Kindle. In that case, just look at the bottom of the book and you'll be able to swipe up to see another menu. On that screen, you'll be asked for your comments. Just let us know what you think!

If that doesn't work, just head over to Amazon or whichever page you bought our book from and you can leave a review on the sales page with ease.

We're truly excited to hear what you think about this book and with your honest feedback, we'll be able to keep reaching out to people and helping them with our content.

Now, all that's left to do is wish you luck and say goodbye!

Made in the USA
Columbia, SC
24 September 2024

42827170R00124